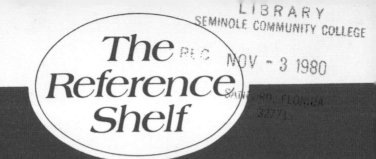

The Reference Shelf

Humans and Animals

EDITED BY

John S. Baky

THE
REFERENCE
SHELF

HUMANS AND ANIMALS

edited by JOHN S. BAKY

THE REFERENCE SHELF

Volume 52, Number 4

THE H. W. WILSON COMPANY

New York 1980

THE REFERENCE SHELF

The books in this series contain reprints of articles, excerpts from books, and addresses on current issues and social trends in the United States and other countries. There are six separately bound numbers in each volume, all of which are generally published in the same calendar year. One number is a collection of recent speeches; each of the others is devoted to a single subject and gives background information and discussion from various points of view, concluding with a comprehensive bibliography. Books in the series may be purchased individually or on subscription.

Library of Congress Cataloging in Publication Data

Main entry under title:

Humans and animals.

(The Reference shelf ; v. 52, no. 4)
Bibliography: p.
1. Animals and civilization. 2. Zoology, Economic.
I. Baky, John S. II. Series: Reference shelf ;
v. 52, no. 4.
QL85.H85   591   80–20577
ISBN 0-8242-0647-9

CONTENTS

III.   ANIMALS IN EDUCATION AND SCIENCE

IV.   THE ANIMAL: PRODUCT OR LIVING RESOURCE

PREFACE

The development of ecology and the popular interest in it suggest that there will be increasing recognition of the aesthetic experience and the physical inter-dependence of the total balanced order of nature. This is an order in which we are parts, not masters; disastrous experience has by now proven (to anyone who might have doubted it) that the old view of nature as intended for human exploitation leads to the suicide of man.[*]

Perhaps not since the middle of the nineteenth century, when Charles Darwin's discovery of the principle of evolution upset the prevailing concepts of human superiority, have so many people been concerned with the fact that humans are first and foremost *animals,* sharing unavoidable, vital relationships with other species. This compilation is intended as a foundation from which the reader can gain a perspective on the diversity and complexity of the relationships that exist between humans and animals—indispensable relationships that we have come to take for granted. We have depended on animals as an important source of food and other products; to be our pets in the home, our servants in the fields, and our prey during hunting season; and to be essential in furthering scientific—particularly medical—knowledge through observation and experimentation. It might be said that humans owe more to other species than those animals owe to us. In any case, the stark fact remains that all other animals, at least in their natural state, can continue to exist quite comfortably without humans, but humans may be doomed without animals.

The opening section furnishes an overview of the natural world and the interaction among species in the delicate ecological balance of the global environment from early times. It is the preservation and maintenance of this balance that demands from humans precise attention to the interdependence of species.

[*] From *On the Fifth Day: Animal Rights & Human Ethics,* by M. W. Fox and R. K. Morris, eds. Acropolis Books. '78. p 23–4.

Section II focuses on the question of whether human needs have priority over animal life. A groundswell of concern has recently solidified into what is known as the "animal rights" or "animal liberation" movement. Thus, a sense of moral awareness on the part of many has begun to force consideration of whether human need (for food, clothing, health, pleasure) justifies the subjection of other species to pain, cruelty, and extinction.

The human-animal relationship is examined from an educational and scientific perspective in Section III, in which some of the articles make the point that information derived from ethology (the study of animal behavior) and investigations of such phenomena as non-human communication have direct applications to human problems.

The commercial use of animals by humans is a practice so taken for granted that we often forget its significance. Section IV approaches this area, first by acknowledging the sheer number of ways that humans depend upon the commercial exploitation of animals, and second by suggesting that many newer forms of exploitation, as well as many traditional ones, are not recognized as ecologically destructive or ethically unjustified.

The critic and naturalist Joseph Wood Krutch once wrote: "The most objective observer . . . cannot help being struck by the change that comes over an animal who has been really accepted as a companion [by a human]. Not only cats and dogs but much less likely animals seem to undergo a transformation analogous to that of human beings who are introduced to a more intellectual, more cultivated, more polished society than that in which they grew up."* The articles in the final section point up the irony that while individual humans often do provide the love and nurture that produce this transformation Krutch describes, our society also tolerates—indeed sometimes promotes—the destruction of animals, by such activities as hunting for sport and the "discarding" of enormous numbers of stray pets.

---

* From *The Great Chain of Life*. Houghton Mifflin. '56. p 133–4.

I. NATURE'S DELICATE BALANCE

EDITOR'S INTRODUCTION

The articles of this section suggest that if we persist in destroying the environment that allows—indeed, requires—all species to make their contributions to the system of organic life, we will soon enter the first phase of a cataclysmic chain reaction that will consume all life on the planet. Awareness of the need to preserve the ecological balance has produced an intense concern and an acceptance of moral responsibility.

In the first article reprinted from *Smithsonian,* Lord Clark, art and social historian, describes the relationship of humans to animals from earliest times to the present. Through art and literature, he traces the changes in man's feelings for animals, from kinship and love to superiority and exploitation. In the second article, also from *Smithsonian,* Dr. Thomas Lovejoy of the World Wildlife Fund ponders the necessity of "environmental triage." As environmental circumstances—mostly manmade—continue to threaten more and more animal species with extinction, we will have to learn how to preserve at least some species while letting others die out, if we are to avoid the loss of virtually all the world's wildlife. In the third article, Julie Ann Miller, writing in *Science News,* describes how mathematical analysis of food webs and environmental factors can reveal basic animal relationships, often hidden by the complexity of plant and animal communities.

The next two pieces, "Leave It to Beavers" by Robert Treuer and "Adapting to Urban Life" by Robert C. Toth, in the Washington *Post* and the Los Angeles *Times* respectively, examine not only the destruction often caused by the natural behavior of certain animals but also how certain animals have survived and flourished through their ability to adapt to environments radically altered by humans.

The sixth selection, entitled "Noah's Ark Is Tomorrow's Zoo," is by Sheldon Campbell, who has been associated with zoos for many years. He notes the process of change in modern zoos, and predicts that "In years to come, zoos will not only be places where animals are exhibited to the public, but repositories where animal species can be saved from extinction. . . ."

"On the Christian Love of Animals," the final selection, is a speech by Professor James Schall, who, in opposition to the arguments of extremists in the animal rights movement, insists on the primacy of man. Couching his argument in a religious context, he advances the proposition that extinction of some species is natural in the grand plan of the evolutionary cycle.

ANIMALS AND MEN: LOVE, ADMIRATION AND OUTRIGHT WAR[1]

The idea that men and animals should live together in harmony lies deep in the human imagination. This dream of a Golden Age recurs in every period of history. There is a leaf from an ivory diptych of the fourth century showing Adam naming the animals; he sits a little apart from them, and is conscious of being a trifle superior, but the animals seem perfectly at their ease and pleased with their names. Then he is joined by Eve; the animals are still there (opposite). There is no sign of fear or hostility. This vision of the Garden of Eden goes back to a far earlier concept that expressed itself in early Greek times by the legend of Orpheus taming wild animals with his song, a myth that occurs in Aeschylus and in the *Bacchae* of Euripides.

Mozart put it into the last and most personal of his works,

---

[1] Article as it appeared in *Smithsonian.* 8:52–61. S. '77. Adapted from *Animals and Men* by Sir Kenneth Clark. Text copyright © 1977 by Kenneth Clark. By permission of William Morrow & Company.

The Magic Flute, in the scene where Tamino plays on his flute and sings so that the animals gather round him (a scene, incidentally, which has nothing to do with the main theme of the opera, and was introduced simply because Mozart loved it).

Did the harmony of the Golden Age ever exist? I am afraid it is unlikely. The reason lies in that faculty which was once considered man's highest attainment, the gradual realization that the sounds he uttered could be so articulated as to describe experiences. He discovered words. Perhaps that, rather than sexual intercourse—which after all is something he had in common with animals—is symbolized by the apple he took from Eve. He could communicate with his fellow men, and so when it came to satisfying his hunger, he could outwit the inarticulate animals: he could tell his fellow men how to dig pits and sharpen swords. The war had begun.

We must remember that primitive man was far closer to the animals than we can imagine. Indeed, he felt—with good reason—that the animals were his superiors. This seems to be the message of the early cave paintings at Lascaux and Altamira. These are popularly known through reconstructions by anthropologists that give an entirely false impression of them. In fact, they are little more than blots and scratches, among which we may recognize undeniable likenesses of bison and other animals. These paintings, say prehistorians, were intended to give men power over animals, and thus increase their success in hunting. But can this be true of the lively and energetic animals that still can be dimly discerned on the uneven walls of Altamira? The few men who appear on the walls at Lascaux cut very poor figures compared with the vigorous animals. Can we seriously believe that these wretched little creatures thought they were gaining power over their magnificent companions? Animals were in the ascendant, and distinguished from man less by their intellectual limitations than by their greater strength and speed. Personally, I believe that the animals in the cave paintings are records of admiration.

The Animal as a Symbol of the Group

The next stage in man's relationship with animals, taking place thousands of years later, seems to confirm my belief. This is the choice of an animal as the sacred symbol of a group: what is loosely called a totem. Hunting for their necessary food and admiring to the point of worship a life-endowment greater than their own, men thus established from the earliest times a dual relationship that has persisted to the present day: love and worship, enmity and fear.

Totemism has existed, perhaps spontaneously, all over the world. But it is in Egypt that we first see totemism turning into what we may call religion. So strong were the vestiges of totemism that in their art the Egyptians continually attempted to integrate man and animal. Men, whose bodies are models of human perfection, retain the heads of birds and animals throughout Egyptian history. These animal heads are an obstacle to our admiration of Egyptian art; the reverse process of the Greeks, which produced the Centaur and the Harpy, seems both biologically and esthetically a more acceptable form of integration. But at a very early date the Egyptians evolved the idea of the sacred animal, the equal and protector of the God King, and sacred animals are the subject of the first pieces of sculpture that can, in the highest sense of the word, be described as works of art.

We may easily feel that there are too many sacred animals in Egyptian art. Yet all of them produced images of great sculptural beauty which gain some of their power from the sacrosanct uniformity of the original idea. Small variations, which may have passed unnoticed by the believer, were due to the fact that these images were made by artists—the Egyptian artist was far from being the self-effacing craftsman of other early civilizations—who knew how to give the prototype the life-giving force of variety.

But, beyond their godlike attributes, the quantity of semi-sacred animals in ancient Egypt owes something to a state of mind that by no means always accompanies religious feeling: love. The Egyptians loved animals. We can see this in the reliefs that decorate tombs around Sakkara. These reliefs show that the Egyptians tried to domesticate animals of all sorts, but succeeded only with those that are our companions today, dogs and cats, and those which still occupy our farmyards. What strange operations of nature have, for 10,000 years, allowed man to domesticate sheep, cattle and horses, but not roe deer?

Cats were pets a thousand years before they were considered sacred (the cult of the sacred cat comes quite late in Egyptian history), and the story in Herodotus that when a house is on fire the first thought of an Egyptian household is to save the cats—"they pass them from one to another, while the house burns down"—is as much a reflection of love as of totemism. The reliefs of animal life in Old Kingdom tombs are inexhaustibly informative and touching. One of the most familiar shows a farmer carrying a calf on his back with the mother cow following and licking it. Where in the Greco-Roman or the Semitic world could such an incident have been sympathetically observed and recorded?

In that other early civilization, which for convenience we may call Mesopotamian, such sentiments could not exist. Ur, Babylon and the other cities accumulated wealth, traded and fought with one another, but insofar as animals entered the Mesopotamian mind, they were symbols of strength and ferocity. The sense of kinship with animals has been superseded by an overawed recognition of their strength, which can be used to symbolize the terrible power of the king.

There is no need to explain why lions and bulls were the semisacred animals of the Middle East. Their strength and potency made them the obvious symbols for a succession of warlike kingdoms. But it is worth recording two or three curious episodes in the history of the bull as a symbol of power. The first is the introduction of the bull as a spectacle in Knossos, in about the year 1500 B.C. Of this, of course, we have no information except what is provided by scanty, and often suspect, visual images. But there is no doubt that a bull was let loose in an arena, where athletes, both male and female, teased it with extraordinary agility. Historians try to interpret this as some kind of religious ceremony, but the Cretans of the second millennium seem to have been less religious-minded than their contemporaries on the mainland, and, in spite of the legend of the Minotaur, I incline to think that it was simply a form of entertainment. If this be so, the bullring at Knossos was something unique in the ancient world, and the forerunner of the Roman amphitheater and the Spanish *plaza de toros*, with the difference that we have no representation of the bull being killed or one of the athletes being gored, although it is almost unthinkable that all of them survived.

The humanizing spirit of Greece treated bulls very differently. It was their potency rather than their ferocity that impressed the Greeks; thus the bull became a favorite embodiment of Zeus, eloping with the not-unwilling Europa, as we see them on a Greek vase.

Propitiating the Gods with Sacrifice

During the 3,000 years in which animals were both sacred and beloved, they were victims of a kind of formalized destruction which now seems to us almost incredible: animal sacrifice. How had this nearly universal practice grown up? Not at first from any urge to kill and destroy. The initial impulses seem to have been more specifically religious: propitiation, atonement and a consciousness of kinship. While men still felt a kinship with animals, to eat them was a crime against the group, and expiation could be achieved only by a ritual feast in which all were involved. Communion was the first basis of sacrifice, as it has remained the last. But quite soon the belief grew up that the gods were pleased by sacrifice. The more the gods had to be propitiated to avert disaster or to secure the success of some enterprise, the more sacrifices they required. The scale of these sacrifices was appalling. When, in the *Odyssey*, Telemachus came to Pylos, he found people on the shore sacrificing jet-black bulls to Poseidon. There were nine companies present and each company had nine bulls to offer. *Les dieux ont soif.*

Thus what had at first been an act of atonement, and even an assertion of kinship, becomes an act of pure destruction, in which animals feed the supposed appetites of a greedy god. And yet when we look at the sacrificial cow from the Parthenon frieze, the "heifer lowing at the skies" of Keats' ode, we are conscious of a certain solemnity. It was only much later, in the desperate effort of the Roman emperor Julian the Apostate to restore paganism, that the Parthenon is said to have stunk like a slaughter house. That a philosophically minded man should have superintended such holocausts shows how much he dreaded the triumph of Christianity.

For it was, of course, Christianity that put an end to animal sacrifice. It also adopted a symbolic animal at the opposite pole from those preceding religions. After the lions and bulls of Mesopotamia and the later cult of Mithras came the lamb and the sheep. Although the lamb is alluded to as a symbol of Christian humility in early texts, it does not appear in art till it can safely be substituted for the hermetic fish. Sheep are the chief symbolic animals of the evolved Christianity of the late fifth century A.D., and inhabit the mosaics of Ravenna, beginning with the beautiful representation of the Good Shepherd in the so-called Mausoleum of Galla Placidia.

But ancient symbolic images are not easily suppressed. The bull, the lion and the eagle make their way back into Christian iconography by a curiously roundabout route. The first vision of the prophet Ezekiel describes an image in terms which are almost incomprehensible, both visually and philologically, but which mention four faces, those of a lion, an ox, an eagle and a man. About 600 years later the author of the Apocalypse, who was so frequently indebted to Ezekiel, speaks of the four beasts that are before the throne of God: "The first beast was like a lion, and the second beast like a calf, and the third beast had a face as a man, and the fourth beast was like a flying eagle." So here they are, our ancient symbolic animals, in a Christian book believed to have been written by one of the Evangelists, a book that had an overwhelming influence in the early Middle Ages: and what could be done with them? The question, like so many in early

Christian doctrines, was answered by St. Jerome. In his famous commentary on Ezekiel he lays it down that these animals are the proper symbols of the four Evangelists—the eagle for St. John, the lion for St. Mark, the bull for St. Luke and the man for St. Matthew. And for more than 700 years almost the only animals in Western art were representations of the Evangelists.

We would like animals to accept our code of moral values (in fact they have moral values of their own), and we love to imagine that they can talk. Children make their teddy bears talk to them, as no doubt did the Egyptian child with its toy hippo and the Greek child with its little bird. These atavistic impulses took grown-up form in a series of writings of which the best known are the bestiaries of the Middle Ages and the fables of Aesop. The bestiaries claimed to give information, and some of it does in fact go back to Pliny. But the greater part is based on legend and folklore. As for Aesop, the fables associated with his name exhibit the same moralizing element as the bestiaries which came much later. The concept that man can learn from the wisdom of animals has a widespread, almost humorous appeal, and revives in a new form the sense of kinship.

Even when the age of symbolic art was over, a few pictures of animals achieve a powerful symbolic quality. One, painted at the high noon of naturalism, is Landseer's majestic stag, "Monarch of the Glen." Nothing in Victorian literature expresses so completely the commanding self-satisfaction of the period. This was no doubt the sentiment of a vast majority. But a small minority, the pre-Raphaelites, took the opposite view, and one of their number, Holman Hunt, expressed it in what is one of the few religious pictures of the age, "The Scapegoat." It was painted with incredible difficulty on the shores of the Dead Sea. Holman Hunt described in detail how he wished to make his goat a symbol of sacrifice, using both the Bible and the Talmud as his sources of inspiration. When it was exhibited, a few critics were disturbed by the expression of Christlike resignation on the goat's face. The majority thought it was just a silly old goat, and could not imagine why Mr. Hunt had gone all that way to paint it.

From Symbolism to Scientific Observation

Long before men had ceased to think symbolically they had begun to think scientifically; that is to say, they had begun to measure and to observe. The first attempt to represent an unusual animal is Matthew Paris' ungainly drawing of an elephant, given by Louis IX to Henry III. But in the mid-13th century a painter was not capable of recording his observations very accurately, and it was only in the late 14th century that one finds real precision.

At the end of the 15th century there appears one of the most skillful portrayers of animals in the whole history of art, Albrecht Dürer. His hand and eye were like the servants of an insatiable curiosity. From his early period comes a monumental crab, a meticulous beetle; then a rhinoceros in full armor; from his last years a walrus with spiny snout, which he saw when he went in search of a gigantic whale that had been washed up in Zeeland, but unfortunately had disintegrated by the time he got there.

As observations, Dürer's drawings of animals have never been equalled. But did he feel anything of the unity of men and animals that is my theme? I doubt it. There was no room for such a sentiment in the man-directed world of the high Renaissance. Indeed, the only artists who saw men and animals bound together by common purposes were those relatively obscure (I believe much underrated) painters, the Bassano family. Jacopo Bassano painted a vast and very detailed picture of one of the great early myths of unity, the entry of the animals into the ark. What a labor of love! Subject and treatment leave one in no doubt that Bassano felt the interdependence of animals and men in a way unknown to any other painters of the Renaissance.

Who can draw the line between animals observed and animals beloved? I suppose that George Stubbs could not have painted horses with so much feeling for their characters if he had not loved them. But he was a classic artist, who did not often show his feelings, and almost the only time he did so is in his picture of a horse called Hambletonian. Hambletonian had been forced to race a famous horse, much his superior, and won the race by a neck, having been cruelly punished by his jockey. It broke his spirit, and he never raced again. All this Stubbs has conveyed with a moving restraint.

The love of animals is sometimes spoken of by intellectuals as an example of modern sentimentality. They have evidently forgotten two passages in Homer which I would have thought unforgettable. The first, in the *Iliad*, describes the horses of Achilles when they learned that their charioteer "had been brought down to the dust by the murderous Hector." Automadon coaxed them and lashed them freely, but the pair refused to move. "Firm as a gravestone planted on the barrow of a dead man or woman they stood motionless, with their eyes to the ground, as they mourned their lost driver." The other is the moment in the *Odyssey* when Odysseus, disguised from Penelope and her suitors, is recognized by his old dog: "There, full of vermin, lay Argus the hound. But directly he became aware of Odysseus' presence, he wagged his tail and dropped his ears, though he lacked the strength now to come any nearer to his master. Yet Odysseus saw him out of the corner of his eye, and brushed away a tear."

But, as you have observed, these passages are about horses and dogs, and there is no doubt that it was through horses, dogs and cats, what we call "domestic animals," that for centuries man maintained his communication with the animals. For some mysterious reason, cats are very rare in European art (in Chinese art they are a favorite subject). But horses inspired Stubbs, to my mind one of the greatest English painters, and the marvelously gifted Géricault, who loved the untamed energy of horses. The procession of dogs in European art is endless, but compared to the dogs of Titian and Velázquez, the dogs in English painting are lightweights. Gainsborough loved a white terrier that belonged to his friend Abel, inflicted it on his sitters, and even painted a portrait of it and its mate. Hogarth loved his dog Trump, which was his constant companion and looks as though it knew a good deal about its master's life.

It is sometimes said that the love of dogs is more intense in England than anywhere else. There are countries where, for no clear reason, dogs are despised. In India and most Moslem countries they lead a dog's life. And even in some Catholic countries they come in for harsh treatment from simple people who have been told that they are without souls. As the Neapolitan says when reproved for beating his donkey: *"Perchè no? Non è cristiano."* I have also known some Englishmen who rebel against the Anglo-Saxon obsession with dogs. They would be shocked by that remarkably intelligent and unsentimental woman, Edith Wharton. Asked to draw up a list of the seven "ruling passions" in her life, she put "Dogs" second, after "Justice and Order." "Books" came third. But in a diary entry she wrote a beautiful modification of her feelings: "I am secretly afraid of animals—of all animals except dogs, and even of some dogs. I think it is because of the us-ness in their eyes, with the underlying not-us-ness which belies it, and is so tragic a reminder of the lost age when we human beings branched off and left them: left them to eternal inarticulateness and slavery. 'Why?' their eyes seem to ask us."

We love animals, we watch them with delight, we study their behavior with an increasing curiosity; and we destroy them. Men have always hunted them with a ritualistic, almost a religious, fervor, which reminds us of our first relationship with them. Animals eat each other, and we eat animals.

But when we pass from the destruction of animals for food to their destruction as a source of money-making, we may be permitted a different stance. In the 17th and 18th centuries the fur trade began to take toll of a wide variety of animals; and in the 19th century took place the most colossal slaughter of all, the attack on the American bison. It is said that 60 million buffalo were reduced to 3,000. Buffalo Bill became a folk hero. As mechanical skills increased, the harpooning of whales became equally menacing to the survival of these intelligent and, for the most part, harmless animals.

In the Middle Ages the relations of men and animals, which had been a haphazard mixture of love, exploitation and destruction, produced a kind of natural balance such as existed in the animal world itself. In the 19th century it became an all-out war. At the same time, those who did not profit directly from killing animals became more sentimentally attached to them, and the knowledge of animal behavior increased to a point undreamed of by earlier naturalists. People became aware that whole species of animals were in danger of being wiped out. The idea of animal conservation appeared just in time; but it will need more than knowledge and devotion if it is to succeed. What is needed is not simply animal sanctuaries and extensive zoos, but a total change in our attitude. We must recognize that the faculty of speech, which has given us power over those fellow creatures whom we once recognized as brothers, must carry with it a proper measure of responsibility. We can never recapture the Golden Age, but we can regain that feeling of the unity of creation. This is a faith we all may share.

WE MUST DECIDE WHICH SPECIES WILL GO ON FOREVER[2]

"You are lucky to catch our springtime," said Sandy Wilbur, endangered species wildlife researcher. "It seems to last only a week here." It had been a dry winter in Southern California, but a vernal spell of excitement and anticipation lay upon the land.

Steep hills and canyons were green with the new growth of the introduced annual grasses that have largely displaced the native perennials. The blue oaks and white oaks were about to be transformed from gnarled wraiths by a new generation of leaves.

The ground was covered with the tiny pink flowers of

[2] Article by Thomas Lovejoy, World Wildlife Fund; one of the nation's prominent wildlife conservationists. Smithsonian. 7:52–9. Jl. '76. © Smithsonian Institution 1976. All rights reserved. Reproduction in whole or in part without permission is prohibited. Reprinted with permission.

red-stemmed filaree, favorite cattle fodder and now part of a California condor food chain because that endangered bird today depends partly on occasional carcasses of cattle instead of those of the formerly resident elk. I had come on behalf of World Wildlife Fund to determine what further efforts might be undertaken to secure the future of America's largest soaring land bird. The condor, now numbering about 50 birds, appears to have reached a state where it has been so interfered with by man that it almost certainly will not survive in the wild without intervention.

There is increasing awareness about endangered species such as the California condor (*Smithsonian*, Mr. '72). The problem is generally confronted on a species-by-species basis: the Mauritius kestrel with nine individuals; the whooping crane with 85 (61 wild birds, 24 in captivity); the Sumatran rhinoceros with fewer than 50. That there are endangered species of plants as well—some 20,000 of them worldwide—is unknown to most. Generally, the whole lot of endangered species seem to be Lewis Carroll creatures with a rather never-never-land existence. It is symptomatic that many people believe the dodo's existence was confined to *Alice in Wonderland*, rather than being one of the first birds exterminated in historic times.

One of the most fundamental units in nature, the species is one of the easiest for the human mind to grasp, unfortunately leading people to think of endangerment and extinction as a series of discrete events, rather than as something that takes place at an estimable rate. Extinction is not only as old as the history of life on our planet, but the usual fate for an overwhelming majority of species. These natural extinctions were usually caused by the evolution of new, more competitive and successful forms of life or by normal environmental change. The extinction rate has fluctuated, but in general it has increased. At the same time, the number of extant species on the planet has continued to increase, with only occasional minor setbacks, until today the total species number somewhere between three and ten million.

At least within historic time, however, and more likely going back into the Paleolithic Age, a new and insidious extinction process has been introduced. In addition to natural ones, man-made extinctions have been occurring—at first quite selectively to eliminate competition or dangerous animals, or by overexploitation of large edible species (it is known prehistoric man caused the disappearance of at least such large animals as the elephant bird or roc of Madagascar and the giant ground sloth of the New World). Increasingly, man has exerted stress, often not deliberate, on the ecosystems of the planet. These systems respond by shedding species just as a plant sheds leaves in response to the stress of drought or cold, and once a species is shed by all the ecosystems in which it naturally belongs, extinction results. The result is impoverishment of the biota of the planet, a reduction of its ability to support man and other forms of life. The problem of endangered species is not, therefore, a hypothetical one, as some may wishfully believe; biotic impoverishment is an irreversible process that has profound consequences for the future of man.

There is no question that extinction rates are accelerating. A graph of historic extinctions of birds and mammals follows the same curve as one for human population growth, but the real extinction rates of historic times are undoubtedly several times higher—because, among other reasons, it is almost impossible to remove a single species from an ecosystem without taking dependent species with it.

Today, with soaring human population increase and with the technological ability to assault nature improving to the point where we are capable of wiping out entire ecosystems, extinction rates are going upward exponentially. This is taking place long before the inventory of the planet's species is anywhere near completion. Scientists have described over a million species—perhaps as many as one and a half million— leaving the job 50 to 85 percent incomplete, depending on what estimate one takes of the total number of species on the planet.

Species are becoming extinct today before they are known to man. Usually we remain in eternal ignorance of what we have lost. Who on receiving a package would toss it out before looking inside? Yet that is what we are doing with our biological heritage.

The tropical forest regions of the globe are some of the richest, both in terms of total species numbers and in terms of undescribed species. Probably only half the fresh-water fish species in the Amazon drainage and fewer than half the soil mites of Amazon soils are known to science. Yet the tropical rain forest is being destroyed at an unprecedented rate. Two-thirds of the southeast Asian rain forests are gone, half of the African rain forests, and more than one-third of the virgin forests of the Amazon have been cut over.

Many of the species of these virgin forests are completely dependent on this primary vegetation and will join the dodo in oblivion if all these forests are cut. Luckily, in the Amazon at any rate, the cutover areas are patchily distributed. Although substantial numbers of described and undescribed species have probably become extinct within the last few years, we have not lost the huge number that would have gone had a contiguous one-third of that forest been cut.

According to one estimate, if all the primary forests of Amazonia were cut, about ten percent of the species stocks of the planet would become extinct. There are current efforts in various Amazonian countries to save some forests, but the results to date are far from adequate; and if the extinctions that have resulted and could result from the assault on the rain forests of Africa and Australasia are also taken into account, it becomes apparent that we are contemplating the loss of a major fraction of the earth's biota. Predictions of extinction rates of 100 to 1,000 times normal by the century's end, and of the extinction of one-quarter or more of all species, no longer seem unrealistic. No one can afford to ignore or dare fail to be disturbed by biotic impoverishment on that scale.

The folly of such profligate handling of our biological heritage is readily apparent if the focus is not on a species-by-species basis, where our abysmal ignorance makes it impossible to ascertain what "good" a particular species might be, but rather on the worth of species in general. Man's egocentric fantasy world continually distracts him from the basic biology of his existence. Species are essential for healthy ecosystems, which in turn are fundamental to the maintenance of the planet's carrying capacity for man and all life. Man, like it or not, is still subject to the process of evolution, and the more that can be learned by studying evolution in nature, the more likely it is that one day he might be able to direct his own evolution wisely. How much the humble fruit fly has taught us! The planet's species also represent a vast genetic resource, the potential benefits of which we have barely skimmed. Many of our domestic animals of today were those of Neolithic Man.

Among the first species to go are large animals, ones requiring large land areas for existence, and often at the end of long food chains. We have little idea of what consequences removing a species at the end of a single food chain would have for an ecosystem.

Many of these first species to go are quite secure under natural conditions, but that very security makes them singularly vulnerable to unnatural disturbance by man. Island species are typical examples; with small populations, they are in equilibrium with their insular environment which, once breached, is too small to afford opportunities for escape. Many of the large animals have a similarly vulnerable security; as species of stable environments, they have evolved to be closely in tune with that stability, and in doing so have sacrificed the ability to recover rapidly from disruption. They live long, begin reproduction late in life and have few young. Whales, whooping cranes, great apes, elephants—all are similarly vulnerable for this reason.

In contrast are the "weed species" which, like crabgrass and dandelions, have the properties of dragon's teeth, almost seeming to thrive on attempts to control or eliminate them. It may seem paradoxical that it is so hard to eliminate species we willfully set about to exterminate. Rats, roaches and mosquitoes are likely to be with us forever, indeed will undoubtedly witness our own extinction. As a consequence, as biotic impoverishment proceeds, the numbers of weed species will remain constant but their proportion of the total flora and fauna will increase. The planet is becoming increasingly a weed patch.

How effective have our efforts been in checking biotic impoverishment? In some terms, the effectiveness has been considerable. The yearly "World Conservation Product" has risen impressively. The Water Quality Act, the Endangered Species Act, the Washington Convention on Endangered Species and many other acts of governments represent tremendous strides. Nonetheless (I would unhappily conclude), in terms of the scale of the problem, we can say with John Paul Jones that "we have not yet begun to fight."

Limited resources of manpower and money are in fact forcing us into employing on a planetary scale an environmental form of triage, the practice evolved by Allied forces in World War I of sorting the wounded into three groups: those likely to die despite medical care, those so lightly injured as to probably recover without care, and the remainder on whom medical resources were concentrated. Should we be deciding on which species and which ecosystems to use our meager conservation resources? And which species and ecosystems should we decide to write off?

Can we possibly save a representative series of species as living museum collections, scattered in various protected ecosystems throughout the world? If this were possible, then once man's mad assault on the natural systems of the planet abates, once the enormous population increases already essentially inevitable are checked and population diminishes to reasonable levels, and if only we haven't spread too many poisons about, *then* might a portion of the planet be reclaimed by the wild? Even given all the ifs, it would not be possible without that representative series. Extinction is permanent, final. Man with all his terrifying ability to destroy species and ecosystems will never have the power to resurrect even a single individual of even one species he has eliminated.

Environmental triage has not been widely practiced in the past. When the numbers of endangered species were small, it did not seem necessary to choose between trying to save the ivory-billed woodpecker or the whooping crane.

With longer and growing lists of endangered species such
choices are being forced. Man's appetite for cellulose is so insatiable it would shame a termite; is it then realistic to try to
save hole-nesting birds such as the Puerto Rican parrot (20
birds) which require large old timber tracts?

Should triage be based on the ease or difficulty with which
a species might be saved? Perhaps we should write off the
most endangered species and concentrate on those for which
our efforts won't be so easily jeopardized by random events.
Would it be wiser to take the $15,000 currently devoted
yearly to the nine Mauritius kestrels and use it to establish a
reserve for the 100 or so St. Lucia parrots, or a reserve for the
pigmy hogs of the Terai of Assam and possibly Nepal, once
thought to be extinct but rediscovered in part through the efforts of Gerald Durrell's Jersey Wildlife Preservation Trust
(*see Smithsonian*, S. '72)? Should we try to save the leopard
rather than the cheetah, because the space needs of the latter
are so demanding? Would the conservation community suffer
a loss of faith if an endangered species were to be deliberately
written off, or is it the only way the point can be made about
the plight of the world's animals and plants?

Genetic considerations certainly play a part in determining how easy it might be to save a species. When a species
drops to low numbers, its genetic variability and flexibility is
considerably constricted. Past low numbers and genetic con-
striction are reflected today in the genetic composition of the
two California elephant seal populations. Lethal and sub-
lethal genes may become prevalent in a remnant population.
Something of this sort indeed is responsible for the low reproductive ability of the major captive breeding stock of the
nene (Hawaiian goose), but happily a few birds with substantial reproductive potential have survived in the wild.

Say Goodbye to the Red Wolf?

On this subject, which is of such importance to captive
breeding and other conservation decisions, we remain woe-
fully ignorant. We know that there are no lethal genes in the

wisent (European bison) population which dropped to less than 200 in the early 20th century, and there may be none in the little Laysan duck of the western Hawaiian islands, which is now known to have had as close a brush with extinction as any sexually reproducing animal can. A female, found in 1930 sitting on a nest of eggs broken by seabirds, fortunately had enough remaining semen from her deceased mate in her oviduct to lay a second clutch. Occasionally, genetic problems of another sort arise, such as those of the red wolf, probably the next American mammal to become extinct unless action is taken. Land-use alterations of forest cover have brought the coyote in contact with the red wolf, and the interbreeding taking place is swamping out red wolf genes with coyote genes. Few red wolves remain.

Sometimes the tumultuous affairs of our own species force a triage. Such would appear to be the case both with the giant sable antelope of Angola and the kouprey of Laos and Cambodia, although our relative inability to do anything for these two species does not automatically imply that the two large ungulates won't survive the current troubled times.

Far more worrisome is that environmental triage is being practiced unconsciously. That the future of the emperor tamarin is relatively secure because of Peru's Manu Park is not totally accidental, but the park was not established as part of a conscious over-all plan to conserve the flora and fauna of the entire Amazon Basin. Colombia's magnificent new Macarena National Park is important in terms of a lowland rain forest park for that country, but will it preclude the reserves for the perhaps 100 endemic bird species in that nation when Macarena itself has not one?

There is a rapidly growing need for a more decisive, more deliberate approach. The Nature Conservancy is consciously attempting to save the full diversity of America's ecosystems. This means, of course, that the Conservancy has essentially written off further New England hemlock groves from its program, leaving any additional efforts to local or other groups. The Conservancy's powerful state heritage program is designed to insure that priority for areas a state is to conserve will go to an ecosystem type not yet protected in that state, rather than duplicate an ecosystem already in an existing reserve.

In South America, the World Wildlife Fund is involved in similar efforts. Costa Rica designed such a priority system a few years ago. A study to identify centers of endemism of the birds of the northern Andes is under way, and a comprehensive effort to establish a master plan for conservation in the Brazilian Amazon will soon be initiated.

In all cases where choices must be made among species, ecosystems and duplication of habitat reserves, we are nonetheless operating in considerable ignorance of what it actually takes to conserve permanently a biological community. Recently, recognizing that most reserves are destined to become islands of natural habitat in a sea of man-dominated environments, theoretical ecologists working on island biogeography have indicated that the very geometry and size of a reserve affects its ability to hold species over time. There is a minimum critical size that must be exceeded in order to guard against heavy loss of species from the reserve. Initial estimates based on rain-forest birds indicate that the lowland forest reserves of South America must be at least 1,000 square miles in extent; the minimum size may be even greater.

The realization has come late; most of the planet's present parks and reserves were established without the minimum-critical-size problem in mind. A number of the areas previously set aside have been large, but they are still far from sufficient. On New Guinea alone 60 percent of the bird species are extinction-prone if large reserves are not established.

Equally disturbing is the effect of fragmentation of unprotected habitats into islands. The spring migration in North America is not only taken for granted, it is big business: the total contribution of bird watching to the Gross National Product in 1974 was 500 million dollars. I can remember being with the Smithsonian's Gene Morton on a spring evening two years ago when, at his call, we were suddenly surrounded by myrtle warblers. An icy thought struck home: there was no reason to assume that this incredible phenomenon of life, of thousands upon thousands of brilliantly colored birds traveling thousands of miles twice each year, would necessarily continue.

My concern then had been about the wintering grounds of the migratory forest birds. Little was known of their needs in this regard, and yet I knew the forest was disappearing rapidly in Latin America. Only recently I learned that the fragmentation of the Eastern deciduous forest is having its own detrimental effect. As the islands of forest become smaller and more isolated from the remaining big patches of forest, the percentage of migratory birds in the summer censuses decline dramatically from around 92 percent in large forests to the 35 percent or lower characteristic of city parks. This process is sufficiently precise for the order in which bird species will be lost to be fairly predictable, with species such as the black and white, the worm-eating and hooded warblers going first.

Everywhere biotic impoverishment seems to be going on even faster. Will conservationists be able to retain their necessary optimism, indeed their sanity?

Later I stood on a high ridge overlooking the Sespe condor sanctuary, a chill damp wind tugging at me as I gazed out toward the condors' last nesting sites. Violet-green swallows and white-throated swifts performed pirouettes on the updrafts of which the condor is so much the master. I wondered what the future held for the condor and other wildlife. If their fortunes could be told, which species had a future? Which must go unheralded, which would go or stay by willful, conscious decisions? Most of all, I found myself in frustration, pondering the imponderable: not *should* such decisions be made, but *why* should they have to be made, as I know they do? Why couldn't there be room for all?

FOOD WEB[3]

Snakes eat frogs and birds eat spiders. Birds and spiders both eat insects. Frogs eat snails, spiders and insects. No wonder ecologists have been caught up in that tangle of relationships they call a food web.

But among the hundreds of food webs naturalists have reported, each based on painstaking observations of a forest, pond or desert, no persuasive patterns have emerged until now, says population biologist Joel E. Cohen of Rockefeller University. "People were just recording—going out and making observations and putting them down."

Ten years ago Cohen, troubled by the limited analysis of ecological data, began studying a branch of mathematics known as combinatorics in the hope of making sense of food webs. He now reports that the web can be untangled into a straight line, or more technically, into a one-dimensional niche space. His analysis demonstrates that the complexities of food webs do not preclude discovering simple patterns that should stimulate further descriptive and theoretical study.

Cohen's analysis pulls together basic concepts of ecology—the food web and the niche space. "This is really the first time we've found a relation between these two fundamental concepts," he says. In his recently published monograph, *Food Webs and Niche Spaces* (Princeton Univ. Pr.), Cohen explains, "By a food web, we mean a set of different kinds of organisms, together with a relation that shows the kinds of organisms, if any, that each kind of organism in the set eats." A niche space, on the other hand, is the composite of all the environmental factors acting on an organism in its natural habitat. Each of these factors, such as temperature or altitude, is considered one dimension of the niche.

Cohen has found that most food webs follow a simple pat-

[3] Article by Julie Ann Miller, life sciences writer. *Science News.* 115:250–1. Ap. 14, '79. Copyright © 1979 by Science Service, Inc. All rights reserved. Reprinted with permission.

tern. According to his mathematical analysis, they depend on only one dimension of the niche. The challenge remaining is to determine just what that dimension is. To confound the problem, that dimension is probably a different characteristic in different communities of organisms. It may be as obvious as animal size—for instance the bigger a bird's beak, the bigger the food it can swallow. Or the dimension may be more subtle, perhaps the ratio of energy gained by eating a prey organism per unit energy expended in predation.

As an analogy, Cohen suggests that geometers trying to classify circles on the basis of size might record the radius, the diameter and area as three separate dimensions of each. Soon, however, such categorizers should realize that only one of those dimensions is sufficient (the diameter is always twice the radius and the area always *pi* times the square of the radius). Similarly, in categorizing communities on the basis of food relationships, Cohen says, "If you classify niches by pressure, temperature, salinity, altitude, humidity and sunshine, a single dimension is sufficient to account for the information in food webs."

Outside the problem of who eats whom, niches may of course have other aspects. For example, a factor that could influence how a community of organisms functions is need for shelter. Going back to the circle analogy, Cohen points out that if the geometers became interested in the color of their circles, the radius dimension would no longer provide sufficient information.

The mathematical idea Cohen applied to the food webs is called an interval graph. Interestingly, this class of graphs was invented twenty years ago by a biologist faced with a very different problem. Seymour Benzer of California Institute of Technology invented the interval graph in an attempt to study the arrangement of mutations within a gene. He found that mutant viruses missing pieces of their DNA could be analyzed so that all the missing segments appeared as intervals of a line. This analysis made it unlikely that the virus's genetic material was arranged in a branched or circular pattern. In this case, in contrast to the food webs and niche spaces, the

one commanding dimension was obvious: It is the physical
linearity of a DNA molecule. (Interval graphs were also invented independently in Europe by G. Hajós as a purely
mathematical speculation.)

Interval graphs since have also played a role in archeology, in which the important dimension is time. Styles of arti-
facts can be associated with an interval of history, so the interval graph helps determine the sequence of findings. The
technique has also been applied in as far-flung fields as psy-
chophysiology, economics and traffic engineering. The idea of
applying it to food webs, Cohen insists, came to him in a
dream after he heard a former classmate define interval
graphs in a lecture.

Although Cohen has done field work in tropical ecology
and primate social behavior, he did not himself collect the
food webs he analyzes. He gathered the 31 webs from descriptions in 22 different papers published between 1923 and
1970. Because many published food webs did not contain sufficient information to be included in his study, Cohen bids
ecologists to be quantitative in reporting their investigations
(for instance, include the actual number of specimens of each
kind of prey taken by each kind of predator under specified
conditions) and to pay particular attention to regions of overlap among predators. So far, he knows of no field investigations specifically designed to test his niche-space hypothesis.
"It takes time for people to digest a new approach," he says.

To explain how he turns a food web into an interval
graph, Cohen works through the example of the community
of organisms living in a Canadian willow forest, reported in
1930 by Ralph D. Bird. In each box of the food web diagram
are organisms that share both predators and prey. The arrows
point from the prey to the predator. Cohen derives from the
diagram a "niche overlap" graph by drawing lines connecting
groups of organisms if and only if both groups have a common
prey. For example, spiders and frogs are joined because they
both eat insects.

The question then is whether all the niche overlaps can be
represented by overlapping intervals of a line. For the willow

forest there are several arrangements of intervals along a line that adequately reflect the observed niche overlaps. For instance, group 2 (a leaf beetle) overlaps only groups 8 and 9 (different kinds of insects). Thus, if in this community the important dimension was, for example, distance from a stream, there would be an area for predation only by those insects.

Cohen further converts the data to tables of 0's and 1's that are convenient for computer analysis. In these tables, a 1 indicates that the predator of the columns eats the prey of that row. From such tables a computer can determine whether the data fit an interval graph. An example of a non-interval pattern is a hypothetical community including four predators (A, B, C, D) in which the only overlaps in diet are between A and B, B and C, C and D and D and A. Such a pattern could not be represented as overlapping intervals along a line.

Twenty out of twenty-three actual single-habitat food webs that Cohen analyzed were found to be interval; the overlaps between predator groups map on a straight line. To see whether that is a surprising finding, Cohen "pseudorandomly" sampled artificial food webs constructed to meet specific criteria. He concludes that the high frequency of interval graphs among the observed food webs is based on something more than chance.

The finding that niche overlaps in food webs can be described by a single dimension of the niche space has three levels of implications, according to Cohen. "It suggests that life may be simpler than one had reason to suspect previously," he says. It also provides a firm basis for other theories of ecology. For instance, theories on the evolution of niches have assumed a one-dimensional niche space as a matter of convenience. A multi-dimensional niche space is simply too difficult to analyze. "That wasn't totally off the wall," Cohen now concludes.

Finally, the analysis provides a new way of looking at things, Cohen says. It should encourage naturalists to look for simple relationships in the confusing complexity of a plant and animal community. Cohen suggests that many of an animal's physiological possibilities may be restricted by the company of other animals. For instance, a bird may have reflexes quick enough to catch a frog, a beak big enough to engulf it and the physiological machinery to digest it. But that is of little import in a natural setting where snakes always get to the frogs first.

Cohen says that he has focused his analysis on food because it is one of the most fundamental themes in ecology: "How to get the energy to survive is basic to how any community works."

LEAVE IT TO THE BEAVERS?[4]

When I first acquired the deserted farm on the banks of the upper Mississippi in the [Bemidji] Minnesota north woods more than 20 years ago, beavers were sparse. Here and there some of the many lodges were occupied. Nearby farmboys and a handful of trappers—and modest fur prices—kept the population in some sort of balance.

I heard stories of the beavers' mischief, flooding roads and inundating farmlands, of neighbors dynamiting dams and trapping them. This sounded needlessly vicious to me, an extreme extension of the ethos of man shaping the world to his convenience at the cost of ecological balance and, ultimately, environmental sanity. My neighbors did not argue, and merely arched their eyebrows, implying that I would learn in time.

The number of beavers declined, until the sighting of an occasional stray in search of terrain and companionship became a rarity. Lakes and creeks are abundant, and the growth of aspen and other foods sought by beavers is rampant, so that it seemed a shame not to have more of them around. This thought came to me often during drought years when water levels dropped and the fire hazard was severe. Then the re-

[4] Article entitled "Leave It To the Beavers? Not By a Dam Site," by Robert Treuer, author of *The Tree Farm* and *Voyageur Country*. Washington *Post*. p E1-2. Ag. 19, '79. © The Washington Post. Reprinted with permission.

tained water backed up behind the beaver dams would have been very welcome; but there were no occupied lodges nearby.

They returned inexplicably in modest numbers, and hard on their heels came the trappers. I posted my land, tried to locate the trappers who came up the river and overland, whose traps and tracks I found but whose ghostlike comings and goings eluded me. I sprang the traps, which they reset. I removed the traps and they sank the swimming raft floating on barrels on my lake with gunfire one day when I was away at work. Then the beavers were gone again, the last lodge trapped out and the conflict became passé.

Game wardens and foresters at the State Department of Natural Resources listened sympathetically to my pleading for the transplanting of beavers into my denuded lake.

"If you have nuisance beavers somewhere and have to trap them, you can put them in my lake," I suggested.

"Live trapping is very time consuming; we don't do that any more," they explained. Where absolutely necessary, licenses were issued to local residents to trap the beavers, killing them and taking their furs. Ordinarily, though, it was a matter of gritting their teeth, planning and building roads and bridges with the possibility of beaver dams in mind and sometimes installing sluices that they opened in the mornings and closed at night, thus baffling the nocturnal beavers as they sought the "leak." No other effective baffles or control have yet been found.

"You're sure you want beavers?" they asked.

"Certainly!" I tend to be emphatic and certain, to my eventual regret.

They returned in numbers and suddenly after a few years. We watched with delight as the old lodge on our lake was renovated and expanded, and two lodges were refurbished on the next lake. It seemed to me that their appetites were modest and their incursions for building materials well within the provender of my woods, without undue damage.

However, they dammed the outlet of the lake, and the water rose ever higher, far beyond their needs. I opened the dam to lower the water level, and they rebuilt it bigger and better by next morning. Woven into the dam structure, amid branches and clumps of mud, was lake bottom debris: cow and pig bones (I had heard tales of farm animals getting mired, then being lost in the silt of the lakeshore long ago), broken glass and pieces of some particularly garish blue and white dinnerware. I did not know the source of these shards, which my wife refers to as Blue Willow. ("Let them haul up the pieces, maybe we can glue them together and wind up with a complete set," she says, but I fail to see the humor; somehow blue and white pieces of plate clash with my image of north woods wilderness.)

After a second and third day of opening the dam, only to find it bigger and better each time than it had been before, I arrived one morning to find it not only rebuilt, but across the top of it a sheet of plastic neatly anchored with branches and mud. I had lost the sheet months before in a windstorm. So much for beavers in the wilds; ours were scavengers pure and simple, too lazy to cut their own dam materials and unearthing human debris and middens as an unsightly labor-saving device. I gave up for the season.

We posted the land and kept a close lookout for trappers in winter, and this time there were no ugly confrontations for there were so many beaver all about that my peculiarity in protecting them did not interfere with the trapping; there were other places for the trappers to go.

It was a long winter, with an unusual amount of snow; with the arrival of warm weather and the spring runoff, the beavers reemerged, their numbers augmented by progeny who had to be taught dam building.

I am told by some neighbors that beavers react to the sound of running water, taking this as a breach of their dikes. If true, this spring's record runoff drove the beavers to heroic efforts of dam building. A tote road, kept open for fire control access, was flooded. The lake expanded in size. The children's swimming hole up the creek became deep enough for my use. The greening trees around the periphery of the lake turned brown as the waterlogged roots rotted and died. The emerald lake was no longer ringed in green, but by brown and sere skeletons of birch, cedar, pine and aspen. Then the access to the building site for our new home became waterlogged and, finally, impassable.

The return of the beavers has produced an unsightly array of dead and dying trees, inconvenience and impediment to our use of the land. In the larger framework of a wilderness ecosystem, with its long-range cycles and episodes, the beavers' presence and alteration of the environment are productive and necessary. On the smaller scale of our land, coexistence—so ardently sought by me for so long—has now become seemingly impossible.

Live-trapping *is* difficult and time-consuming.

Operating a sluice installed in their dam—opening it in the morning and closing it in the evening—becomes a major chore, and represents an installation expense.

Dynamiting the dam, which frequently drives out the beavers, or trapping (killing) them go against my grain.

I amuse friends by describing the recipes I intend to use for Christmas dinner of roast beaver, and my plans to make a beaver coat for my wife ("But I want a storebought coat!" she expostulates).

Meanwhile, our house-building project is stalled, no alternative sites being feasible, and more trees around the lake are dying. I grit my teeth while they whet theirs. I contemplate beavercide while my children, groomed and conditioned to a love of wildlife over the years, tell me that the young beavers are "cute" and of watching them at close range.

Tonight an engineer is to visit to advise me on the cost of building a bridge.

ADAPTING TO URBAN LIFE[5]

Interstate highways with multiflora rose shrubbery planted in their median strips as car barriers have lured

[5] Article entitled "Wildlife Is Moving Into the Cities," by Robert C. Toth, reporter, Washington bureau. *Los Angeles Times.* p N3. O. 22, '78. © 1978 The Los Angeles Times. All rights reserved. Reprinted with permission.

southern mockingbirds as far north as Maine. The birds feed on the rose pips throughout the coldest winters.

Coyotes from the West have spread across the breadth of the country into the Appalachian Mountains. They are "in residence," authorities say, in such cities as Chicago, Cincinnati and Albany, N.Y.

Alligators, although an "endangered species" whose killing is strictly limited, have attacked dogs and children in Florida and Louisiana. They have stopped street traffic, and have turned up on front lawns, even in homes.

There was a time, not too long ago, when wildlife experts feared that creatures like the mockingbird—if not the coyote and alligator—were being driven farther and farther from American cities as each new load of concrete and lumber further expanded municipal boundaries. Soon, it was feared, urban Americans, who make up 70 percent of the population, would see wildlife only on their television sets—and then maybe only in animated cartoons.

But the trend has not been that way. On the contrary, more and more wildlife is showing up in U.S. cities. Experts say some of the reasons are:

—A warming climate. Among other things, this has caused the northward "explosive" migration of the Virginian opossum, a grizzled marsupial that uses its hairless tail as an extra arm or leg.

—A lack of natural predators in urban settings—which has contributed to another exploding population species, the raccoon. Equally at home in old trees and new chimneys, feeding from tipped garbage cans at night, the raccoon persists despite threats from such enemies as cars, youths with air rifles and an occasional brave dog.

—Anti-pollution drives. In Washington, an extensive cleanup of the Potomac River has returned beavers to the waterway, even in the vicinity of the capital.

Building New Habitats

But most important is the amazing tolerance and adaptability of many kinds of creatures to man and his urban civilization. Despite his constructions, and sometimes thanks to them, more animals than expected are surviving in urban environs, both silent and raucous, benign and harmful, intriguing and plain nuisances.

A peregrine falcon has established its scrape, or nest, on a downtown Baltimore bank building. She is the latest of her kind attracted to a skyscraper aerie by the fast-food promises in plump, slow pigeons. Falcons have also been found living in Chicago, New York, Boston, Philadelphia and Harrisburg.

Sloppy carpentry in new housing developments in Maryland that left unboxed eaves and unscreened louvers has created nesting spaces that now attract hordes of starlings and house sparrows. One wildlife researcher is said to be able to identify the builder of tracts in the new town of Columbia according to the number of birds living in the crevices.

Storm drains, railroad banks and other conduits have made it relatively easy for wildlife to enter cities from rural regions. Interstate highways also permit easy migration from region to region.

The mockingbird moved throughout the Northeast in just eight years, according to Richard M. De Graaf, an Agriculture Department wildlife research biologist. While the rose shrub was responsible in that case, other animals are moving under cover of crown vetch, a flowering plant used to minimize erosion on highways' steep sides.

The energy crisis of the past five years has also affected the wildlife population and its movement into new locales.

Rising gasoline costs have forced highway maintenance crews to reduce mowings along federal and state roads, permitting higher grass and brush cover for wildlife, according to Thomas M. Franklin of the Urban Wildlife Research Center.

Thus, ring-necked pheasants and voles, a dumpy looking field mouse, have proliferated and moved into the Northeast and the Midwest, he said. The voles, in turn, attract predatory birds. What is more, motorists in these areas say they increasingly spot gracefully circling sparrow hawks, red-tailed hawks and small falcons.

Adapting to City Life

Wildlife in urban settings sometimes adapt not only their behavior but also their physiology to the new environment.

In England, for example, one species of moth has changed from the white to black-winged variety, apparently to fit and survive better against sooty backgrounds. Blackbirds have been heard singing at night in London, perhaps because of the lights. Due to city warmth, they also are said to produce young 10 to 14 days earlier than rural blackbirds.

Foxes now have dens in every major American city in their climate zone. (There was even one under the bleachers of Yankee Stadium, John Rublowsky wrote in his book, *Nature in the City.*) But urban foxes seem to have duller senses, and they breed as much as three months earlier than their country cousins, researchers say.

The hedgehog, a porcupine-like creature in England that curls up and lies still when sensing danger, has begun to modify its behavior to cope with the automobile. Instead of playing possum, it now runs at the sound of an engine.

Animals in cities sometimes get urban diseases. Dogs in Philadelphia, for example, get cancer of the tonsils more often than their equals in adjacent rural regions.

Various types of urban wildlife can be health hazards to humans—from cockroaches, bats and rats to wild (and sometimes domestic) dogs and cats. Even aesthetically pleasing animals can be destructive to shrubs and structures. With rising numbers, they become real pests.

Imported Trouble

Many of the wildlife nuisances have intriguing histories.

Three of the peskiest birds—pigeons, house sparrows and starlings—were all deliberately imported to this country, for example.

Irridescent, pugnacious starlings, whose flocks darken the sunset in many big cities, are . . . [progeny] of 60 birds released in 1890 in New York's Central Park by a man who wanted all of the birds mentioned in Shakespeare's writings to be found in North America.

Starlings are commuters in reverse, feeding in fields by day but preferring urban settings at night. They have pushed out bluebirds and other songbirds from nests, and are even said to have ousted desert birds from nests in cactuses in the Southwest.

Similarly, the perky, curious house sparrows of today came from a single flock released in Brooklyn in 1852, for no known reason. The sparrow population peaked when the horse was the main engine of transportation, since feed grains, straw and even flies were conducive to its flourishing.

The ubiquitous pigeon arrived with early settlers in the 1700s, perhaps to carry messages for the military or just as pets. It survives because of its great fertility and because it eats almost anything.

Also imported have been some exotic wildlife which accidentally got loose to become dangerous pests, mostly in Florida where the climate is hospitable.

Some 50 such animal species have been counted, according to the National Geographic Society. They include giant Colombian iguanas, walking Siamese catfish—2-inch-long creatures with stiff fins that permit them to "walk" across roads—and the Amazon flesh-eating piranha, brought in under strict control but freed by careless handling.

Even rhesus monkeys, imported for early Tarzan films and later freed, survive in Florida swamps as curiosities.

In Florida, too, are western jackrabbits which escaped in 1940 from a training farm for racing greyhounds and which now have descended on the state's cattle ranches.

Armadillos, descendants of escapees from a private zoo in Cocoa Beach, Fla., that was destroyed in a 1924 hurricane, roam the Florida countryside. These animals, which ruin lawns by boring under them, are also invading from Mexico. They already are found in the Gulf states and as far north as Tennessee.

NOAH'S ARK IN TOMORROW'S ZOO[6]

Zoos of one kind or another are among the most ancient of man's institutions. As long ago as 2500 B.C., Egyptian potentates had zoos or animal farms at which they kept hyenas, monkeys, mongooses, ibex, antelope and other animals. Throughout most of their long history, zoos have been places where animals have been caged or penned so that people could look at them.

These days, though, zoo directors are redefining their purpose. Many zoos are in the process of changing, and they can be expected to change even more in the future. In years to come, zoos will not only be places where animals are exhibited to the public, but repositories where animal species can be saved from extinction through captive breeding.

Animal Sanctuaries

The most powerful force influencing the future of many animals—and of zoos—is the decline of the wild. Not even zoo directors would argue that zoos are better places for animals than the fields and forests of their native lands, yet zoos, public or private, may be the last chance for some creatures that would otherwise pass quietly into oblivion. The world's population will increase from four billion to seven billion by the early years of the 21st century. Animal species like the Norway rat will prosper, but many animals, caught in the crush, are apt to disappear forever. On every continent except Antarctica forests have been cut to provide building materials and charcoal, or cleared for farms and houses, while the homes of the original inhabitants, from ants to Indians, have been destroyed. As the trees have fallen and new dams

[6] Article entitled "Noah's Ark in Tomorrow's Zoo: Animals Are A-Coming, Two By Two," by Sheldon Campbell, associated with zoos for forty years. *Smithsonian*. 8:42–51. Mr. '78. © Smithsonian Institution 1978. All rights reserved. Reproduction in whole or in part without permission is prohibited. Reprinted with permission.

have filled valleys with water, unique animals have been left homeless: lemurs on Madagascar, pygmy hippopotamuses in West Africa, tapirs in Central and South America, orangutans in Indonesia and many more.

There is a thin, red line of designated reserves and national parks in which our animals can find sanctuary, but even these havens are sometimes reduced in size—or simply overrun. In the Gir Forest of India, next to a reserve established to save the last Asiatic lions graze domestic cattle whose owners want the lions destroyed. Similar conflicts are now taking place along the borders of most game reserves in Africa.

In the past, zoos themselves have contributed to the decline of animal populations. Through most of their history zoos were "net users" of animals, taking from the wild more than they gave to the world. New animals were cheap, so cheap that a few unscrupulous zoo managers chose to let some species die each year rather than incur the costs of building larger, more humane exhibits, installing heated quarters or breeding pens, or giving special attention to diets. This exploitation continued until 20 or 30 years ago, when zoo directors began to realize that, on the one hand, animals are complex beings with needs beyond food and water, while on the other hand the wild was disappearing and would not be available for replenishing stocks.

Even then there was ample evidence to indicate that zoos could save animals from extinction. Père David's deer, a splendid creature with broad hooves and a rather long tail, disappeared from the wilds of its native China perhaps 3,000 years ago, but it still survives—in zoos. It is doubtful that many (or any) of the stocky, short-legged Przewalski's horses, the world's only surviving wild horse, still roam the plains of Mongolia, but 200 or more are alive and well—in zoos.

Captive Breeding

Starting after World War II, some forward-looking zoo administrators began seeing zoos in a new role, in effect as conservation banks, places where endangered species could be held in trust. At the Basel Zoo in Switzerland, Dr. Ernst Lang began 25 years ago to select endangered species specifically for breeding. At the Bronx Zoo (New York Zoological Park), the director, William Conway, formulated an intellectual base for captive breeding and began to reduce the number of species displayed in order to have more breeding groups. The San Diego Zoo's Dr. Charles R. Schroeder energetically pushed the development of the 1,800-acre San Diego Wild Animal Park as a breeding area for larger animals. In East Berlin, Dr. Heinrich Dathe started the Tierpark in 1954 with the idea that it should be a "paradise" for animals—including such rarities as the Asiatic lion. In 1959, animal collector and author Gerald Durrell started his Jersey Zoo on the largest of England's Channel Islands with the intent of breeding smaller, often neglected creatures.

Though there were many difficulties to surmount, these early efforts at captive breeding soon began to pay off. The most spectacular success had to do with an animal called the Arabian oryx, a large, beautifully marked antelope with spectacular spearlike horns. The oryx, which was probably the source of the unicorn legend, has traditionally scrabbled its living from sparse desert plants amid the sand and rock of the Arabian peninsula. Since it was the largest game animal in modern Arabia, a hunting mystique grew up around it. Sheikhs eagerly set out to kill their oryx the way Masai warriors once sought lions. A successful hunt, which meant a dead oryx, was identified with manhood. In the days of horses and muzzle-loaders the animals held their own, but when Jeeps, helicopters and rapid-fire weapons came upon the scene the oryx, never numerous, quickly began to disappear.

Fortunately, anticipating the species' demise, in 1962 the Fauna Preservation Society with the World Wildlife Fund set up a program to capture some of the few animals then left. A thrilling and dangerous hunt produced two males and one female. These, with a second female from the London Zoo, a third female donated by the ruler of Kuwait, and two more pairs from the King of Saudi Arabia, were placed in the hot, dry Arizona desert at the Phoenix Zoo as a "world herd." On nine animals, essentially, hung the future of an entire species. To make the situation more of a cliff-hanger, the first seven offspring were males.

Later, though, females were born, the herd began to prosper, and, to date, there have been 71 births, enough to have started new herds at the San Diego Wild Animal Park and the Gladys Porter Zoo in Brownsville, Texas. The breeding effort came just in the nick of time, because for several years now, no live wild oryx have been reported on the Arabian Peninsula—but within the next year or so they will be seen there again, when animals from the Phoenix herd are returned to a preserve in Jordan.

In the future, as zoos stress captive breeding more and more, zoo administrators and staffs are going to confront problems that they have not traditionally had to face. The foremost problem is simply this: it is often difficult to get animals to mate in captivity. To the public, the problem of breeding wild animals may seem no problem at all. Put male and female together at the right age and soon they will multiply and replenish the Earth. But in fact so little is known about the habits of many species that they have been kept paired in zoos for years without producing offspring.

Copulation must take place at an optimum time in the sexual cycles of both male and female, and sometimes only as one action in a complex set. A male animal may be indifferent to one consort but stimulated by several. He may require ritualized combat with another male before he is aroused, and then he, victorious, may be snubbed by a female who has found another victorious male more attractive. Esoteric diet supplements may be needed to provide what amounts to an aphrodisiac. Or the animals may need exercise, space to perform courtship dances, a place to be alone, or even training in copulatory techniques.

The complexities involved in captive breeding are evident in the case of the golden marmoset, a lovely little Brazilian monkey with a yellow, lionlike mane. Since 1965 scientists have been trying to improve the breeding success of the golden marmosets at the Smithsonian's National Zoological

Park in Washington. In early attempts at the National Zoo and other institutions, the zoologists found that captive-born parents ignored, abused and sometimes inadvertently killed their offspring. After considerable observation, the scientists learned that the female and male both had to have experience living with and helping to care for younger siblings *before* they themselves became sexually mature—that is, marmosets could successfully rear their young only if they had had early experience in a family situation. But that discovery was only the beginning.

The researchers also learned that if young marmosets are left with their family groups for *too* long—four or five years—they are unlikely to breed. Other research showed that the animals needed special diets if they were to produce offspring. Instead of the carbohydrate-rich fruit diet they were customarily fed, they required a menu high in protein. In 1977 the National Zoo achieved its greatest success when 17 golden marmosets were born and raised.

At Front Royal, Virginia, the National Zoo's Research and Conservation Center, scientists found a quite similar set of problems—and a different solution—in working with the maned wolf, an endangered South American animal that resembles a giant, long-legged fox. Since in captivity maned wolves have generally not cared for their pups, the practice has been to "pull the pups" for hand rearing. But the Front Royal researchers came up with a better answer when they realized that the wolves were extremely shy, and that the mothers needed isolation both from other animals and prying human eyes. (At Front Royal, animals are not displayed to the public, and even scientists try to remain unobtrusive so as to give the animals a sense of being in a wild state.)

The researchers tried an experiment. They used closed-circuit television cameras to monitor the birth of a wolf litter so that there was no human presence to disturb the mother. Feeding was carried out by keepers who ran in and threw down the food, then withdrew quickly. Left alone and undisturbed, the wolf proved to be a good and caring mother.

To carry out such captive breeding programs on a large

scale in the future, zoos will have to confront some other problems that have nothing to do with the animals themselves. For one thing, coils of recent legislation directly affect the breeding of endangered animals. Under a convention signed in 1973, one nation after another has established laws designed to prevent the removal of endangered animals from their native countries for any purpose. In order to capture an Indian elephant in the wild for transport to the United States, a zoo now requires permits from both governments and supporting documents the size of a small-town telephone directory.

Red tape also creates difficulties when zoos try to sell endangered animals to one another. Shipments have to be justified and permits obtained to send an endangered species from the Basel Zoo in Switzerland to the Philadelphia Zoo, or for that matter from Philadelphia to Los Angeles. Zoos can avoid the red tape by giving or lending animals to one another, options that they often choose. But if captive breeding is to be successful, they must also be able to sell surplus animals to help pay for their breeding programs.

An additional complication is a host of laws in every country that prevent the importation of diseased animals or animals which may escape, propagate and severely disrupt native ecosystems, as the mongoose has done in Hawaii and goats nearly everywhere. In the United States these laws have recently been beefed up. Traffic in all exotic birds has several times been brought to a virtual standstill because of outbreaks of Newcastle disease, a threat to poultry raisers. And no wild swine—forest hogs, warthogs and others—can be shown in American zoos because the Department of Agriculture has a ban on their importation for fear that they might introduce African swine fever.

Zoo directors are, of course, sympathetic to the aims of such laws protecting endangered species and preventing the spread of disease, as long as the amount of red tape is kept to the necessary minimum, but sometimes it is not. Bureaucratic delay in issuing a simple form by one of three nations involved held up for several weeks the transfer of a male Komodo dragon from Europe to join two females for a breeding program in the United States.

Another obstacle to captive-breeding programs is the feeling on the part of a segment of the public that zoos in general should be abolished. In the minds of many people there remains a stereotype drawn from the dreadful image of the 19th-century menagerie—a barred prison whose inmates spent miserable lives of frustration and boredom. This image is kept alive by the continued existence of roadside and other private zoos where animals live in foul, cramped cages. One antizoo organization's "investigative report," with the alliterative headline "Torment, Torture and Terror Close in on Zoo Animals," states: "It's time to phase out zoos. It's time to liberate zoo animals from exploitation by not replacing those that die. It's the only way to save them from being made abnormal by animal behaviorists whose objective is modification—the alteration of the animal's natural behavior."

In fact, research being done in zoos today is directed toward relieving the conditions most frequently attacked. The effort is to better the lot of captive animals by conquering diseases or by understanding behavior, so that exhibits can be better designed, correct diets used and propagation achieved. Behavior modification has indeed been used—to correct behavior that is unnatural. At the San Diego Wild Animal Park, for example, behavior modification was used to teach a female gorilla the techniques of motherhood.

Perhaps what disturbs zoo directors most about anti-zoo criticism is that it comes from people who truly care about animals, and whose energy, influence and financial support could help a great deal in captive breeding programs.

Indeed, financial support—or the lack of it—is one of the most serious problems zoo directors face. Some conservationists feel that instead of merely breeding animals in captivity, zoos should devote some of their resources and revenues to restoration of wilderness areas. The fact is, though, that zoos have been hit so hard by inflation that what money there is must be used not for wilderness conservation, but for animal conservation. Food for animals has gone up at the same rate as food for people. Fodder to supply one elephant for a year now costs around $750, up 20 percent from 1973. Meat eaters are even more expensive. Food for one tiger costs $1,650, up 28 percent. Construction costs have soared, making new exhibits two or three times as expensive as they were five years ago.

Despite their concern for endangered species, few conservation organizations have stepped in to support captive-breeding programs. Because their main efforts are primarily directed toward protecting animals in remaining wilderness areas, organizations like the World Wildlife Fund and the National Wildlife Federation are inclined to think of zoos only as a last resort, as in the case of the World Wildlife Fund's helping to save the Arabian oryx. Indeed, an officer of one prominent conservation society once said that he would rather see the California condor extinct than made captive for breeding.

Problems notwithstanding, zoo directors still feel reasonably confident that they can increase and improve captive-breeding programs and, while they are at it, change the image of zoos in general. In the future, zoos are apt to exhibit more animals of fewer species in order to provide the space for captive breeding. Nowadays many zoo directors question the desirability of exhibiting in the old manner several subspecies of the same animal. Because all tigers look very much alike, there is little need today to display side by side the Bengal, Siberian and Sumatran subspecies.

There will be much greater emphasis on research directed toward curing animal ills and understanding animal behavior. Behavioral studies of confined animals will lead to better exhibits for both animals and viewers. Minute changes in an exhibit, when they are based on an animal's biological imperatives, often produce astonishing results. For example, climbing animals like to have places to climb to. Space in a monkey exhibit can be "enlarged" psychologically by putting in screens that enable individuals to isolate themselves from the eyes of cage mates and the bold stares of human primates outside.

Biomedical researchers will concentrate on diseases of exotic animals, many of which are poorly understood. No matter how large the zoo, animals live in concentrations not found in nature. Newborn animals are particularly susceptible to umbilical infections spread by vectors that would normally be dispersed widely in the wild. Viral diseases, spreading rapidly, can literally wipe out a herd or flock.

Zoo designers will deal with a four-faceted problem: each new exhibit will have to allow natural behavior by animals, strike the visitor as meritorious beyond merely showing the animal, be readily accessible for keepers and veterinarians, and be constructed with a sharp eye for cutting costs. Where some of the more elaborate preinflationary exhibits were like stage sets for *Aida*, future exhibits will probably make do with a few scene-setting props in the manner of *Our Town*.

Zoos in the future are going to cooperate much more than they have in the past, exchanging information and animals for captive breeding. Already there are more and more "breeding loans" of a single male or female animal, not only to obtain young but to reduce the genetic defects from inbreeding. Zoo directors are beginning to talk of establishing cooperative programs for selected endangered species, particularly those most difficult to breed. Several zoos in a consortium would jointly plan the program, treating individual animals as though they were communally owned and sharing in the results. The program to save the Arabian oryx will provide the model. Trustees of the world herd meet at least once a year to discuss results and reset objectives. Presently those zoos with herds of Przewalski's horses are moving toward a consortium-like arrangement, and zoos in the British Isles are establishing consortia for breeding the great apes.

In the future, major zoos will be trustees for several endangered species. Smaller zoos may breed one or two species, participate in consortia, or simply act as outlets for surplus animals. In fact, a major zoo might supply animals, consultation in exhibiting and veterinary services for small zoos in its geographical area.

Technology will play an ever-increasing role. Because

breeding loans involve risks, trauma, adverse reaction to drugs used in capture guns and injury during shipment, many zoo professionals are anxious to see artificial insemination more widely used. Then only sperm need be shipped. So far, research has not solved all the problems. At Cornell University, biologists have been extremely successful in inseminating hawks, but a London Zoo program with an elephant has encountered difficulties. Working with African game authorities, the zoo's biologists have taken sperm from bull elephants immediately after they have been shot in cropping programs and rushed it, deep-frozen, to London to inseminate a captive female—but no pregnancy has yet resulted. Still, artificial insemination should become more dependable in the future and, looking ahead, the San Diego Zoo has already installed a cell bank, a "frozen zoo," where cell and sperm samples from endangered animals can be kept against the day when insemintion or cloning might be used to re-create a species all but extinct.

Another technological aid to captive breeding will be the ISIS (International Species Inventory System) center in Minnesota. Sponsored by the Department of the Interior and American Association of Zoological Parks and Aquariums, ISIS will be a computerized inventory, with sexes and bloodlines, of all vertebrate species in most North American zoos and a few in Europe. When the programming is complete, zoo managers will be able to obtain printouts that locate and identify captive animals in all participating zoos.

The objective of many breeding programs is the return of animals to the wilderness, as is planned with the oryx. But the fact is that the zoos are likely to become the final reserves for some species. Few conservationists even dream of returning big predators like lions and tigers to their old haunts. Training such animals to hunt would be difficult and no thanks would come from farmers or herdsmen in areas where the predators were released. Fewer than 300 Siberian tigers are thought to survive now in the wild. More live in zoos, where they are likely to remain.

As a last berth in the ark for many animal species, the

zoos of the 21st century will become much more important than they have ever been in the past. Species driven to the brink of extinction will be preserved for generations to come. And perhaps something more than the animals will be saved. As the wild declines, in zoos it may be modeled in miniature—a tropical rain forest, a Galápagos island, a Serengeti plain—bringing to visitors a taste of wilderness, the flavor of a world that used to be. Then the animals, according to their natures—in families, troops, flocks and herds—will become actors creating on an appropriate stage a willing suspension of disbelief, so that harried people can leave civilization behind and in the re-created wilderness be once again primitive man in a primitive world.

ON THE CHRISTIAN LOVE OF ANIMALS[7]

To be human is to be concerned about animals. Man is the social *animal*, the animal which laughs, as Aristotle said. Very often, our notion of this animality in us is looked upon as something rather evil and frightening. Animal images are often used as descriptions of our actions at their humanly worst. Animals, acting like animals, are functioning well and properly, doing what they are made to do. Lacking better terminology, perhaps, we say that men at their worst are "bestial," though in justice to Aristotle who used such wording, care was taken to note that animals were supposed to be bestial, were supposed to act according to their own natures. Plato, in a famous analogy in *The Republic*, warned of that wild, untamed, reckless animal deep within us revealed by our dreams and too often by our actions. In an oft-quoted phrase, Thomas Hobbes claimed that "man was a wolf to

[7] Speech entitled "On the Christian Love of Animals; the Worst of Us Is Better Than the Best of Them," by James V. Schall, associate professor, presented to the faculty and student body of the University of San Francisco. *Vital Speeches of the Day.* 43:81–6. N. 15, '76. Copyright © 1976 by City News Publishing Company. All rights reserved. Reprinted with permission.

man," whereas wolves apparently are quite kindly beasts in general. And Descartes even proposed that animals were machines because we could hypothesize that they might be.

But the subject of animals, our treatment and use of them, and our relation to them has suddenly been repropounded from a number of diverging sources. Generally, in the Judaeo-Christian tradition, animals were held to be under man's "dominion." This meant that the animal kingdom was for man's use and well-being. Men were not to be sacrificed to animals. Currently, however, the ecology school warns us that we must not tamper further with our bio-physical environment. The cycle of plants and animals is vital to humanity. E. F. Schumacher, in his widely discussed, *Small Is Beautiful*, insists from an economic view that we must learn to live with the animals again, to stress permanent and rooted things. "For man to put himself into a wrongful relationship with animals, and particularly those long domesticated by him," Schumacher wrote,

has always, in all traditions, been considered a horrible and infinitely dangerous thing to do. There have been no sages or holy men in our or in anybody else's history who were cruel to animals or who looked upon them as *nothing but* utilities, and innumerable are the legends and stories which link sanctity as well as happiness with a loving kindness towards lower creatures.

Peter Singer and Thomas Regan are intellectual leaders of a vast revisionist movement known as "Animal Liberation" which purports to carry the Black, Gay, and Woman's Liberation Movements to their logical conclusions. They insist that we take a look at the vast amount of pain we inflict on animals by our factory farms, our hunting practices, our zoo keeping facilities, our treatment of pets, our experimentations, our use of pelts, eggs, and meat. English Roman Catholics have a study group devoted to animals, a group which maintains a kiosk of information at Lourdes and has even made a pilgrimage to Rome in the name of animal care. They also publish a journal, not unexpectedly called, *The Ark*. And the proliferation of health food stores and Buddhist monks all over the West attest to the arrival of a new ethic and attitude towards nonhuman life. We may very well be at the state of a total restructuring of society that would follow from our accepting what Albert Schweitzer called, "The Ethic of Life," life in men, animals, insects, and plants. In short, this may not be such a propitious time to invest in Armour, Dubuque, or Jimmy Deane's Pork Sausage, but rather in General Mills and Iowa soybean land.

In this context, I wish to raise the question, paradoxical as it sounds, of the Christian love of animals. Oddly, I have learned that in our society no two subjects are more emotionally explosive than criticism of animals and criticism of abortion. At first sight, I never felt the two were particularly connected, but now I am inclined to think that they are. Indeed, I suspect the animal liberation movement may be the best ally the abortion critics can have. This has not been apparent so far since most Christians have felt the animal liberationists prefer animals to humans. But this need not be the case. A growing respect for all life cannot help but result in a respect for human life in all its forms. And this too may well be a positive thing in the attempts to improve the diets of men all over the world.

There are, however, levels of theory and levels of manners and practice. Christianity has not neglected the animals. In the Gospel of Luke, Christ asks, "Are not five sparrows sold for two pennies? And not one of them is forgotten before God. . . . Fear not; you are of more value than many sparrows." The notion of human dominion did not mean, then, that single sparrows were not within God's concern, even though men and women might be of more value than a flight of sparrows. And we read in *The Little Flowers of Saint Francis of Assisi:*

A certain youth had caught one day a great number of turtle-doves; and as he was taking them to market he met St. Francis, who, having a singular compassion for these gentle creatures, looked at the doves with eyes of pity, and said to the youth: "Oh good youth, I pray thee give me these gentle birds, to which in the Holy Scriptures chaste and humble and faithful souls are compared; and do not let them fall into the hands of cruel men who would kill them" (London, Kegan Paul, 1905).

What, then, are the implications of a Christian love of animals within this broader context of concern for life, animal liberation, and the fact that men are worth more than many sparrows?

To place myself firmly in the context of human manners rather than the more metaphysical issues that will arise later, I am frankly biased about animals—unfavorably biased. Let me begin by noting that I am not amused with friends' furry spaniels or their slinky cats jumping all over me in what is wildly called "enthusiastic greeting," when I am invited into their homes. "Love me, Love my dog" I definitely consider an immoral principle. In my jaundiced view, it must either be, "Love me, Contain your pooch" or else, "Love your Puddles, Look for a new friend." When Aristotle said that man was a "rational animal," he meant, at a minimum, that the worst of us is better than the best of them. Thus, I fully admit to receiving an occult pleasure every time I see W. C. Fields' famous remark, "Anyone who hates dogs and children can't be all bad." Now, I happen mostly to like children. Some, to be sure, are quite obnoxious little critters. I am no absolute idealist. But I do not consider Field's law to be one whit less valid for all that I am perfectly willing to stand on the validity of the thus truncated remnant.

Further, I confess, along with any honest believer, that I have as much trouble as anyone else in observing the Ten Commandments, not to mention those Two Great Summaries which contain the Law and the Prophets. However, I have no difficulty whatsoever in obeying the admonition in the *Book of Leviticus* which reads:

> Every swarming thing that swarms upon the earth is an abomination; it shall not be eaten, whatever goes on its belly, and whatever goes on all fours, and whatever has many feet ... you shall not eat for they are abominations.

But *No Way* are you going to catch me munching caterpillars, night crawlers, hornets, or ants—even if the Japanese do cover them with chocolate. In my book, there is absolutely no need for a special revelation on these matters.

Consequently, to return to what some optimists describe

as "Man's Best Friend," I do not appreciate the automatic assumption that I ought somehow to be enthralled by my friends' basset hound or by one *Samba*, an obnoxious beast of no particular breeding, distinctive only in that she bites strangers frequently, as if mutts somehow transcend the human decency of requiring time and evidence of friendly intent and physical attraction before we are able to conceive any sort of affection for them. I am tired of visits in which the entire intellectual content of my brilliant conversation consists in repeating over and over in a weak voice, "Nice Doggie." This is especially difficult during my annual half year in Rome where I am not at all sure dear *Fidone* with the snarling teeth at all understands my American accented version of "Down Boy."

"Dogs," I am frequently reassured, "can tell whether you like them or not." Well, I say, the feeling is mutual. And just how this philosophic tid-bit about an audibly growling dogdom, which perfectly well knows that I hate its guts aids in my legitimate right of self-defense, I have never quite been able to figure out.

Furthermore, I hate smelly animals in nice houses though I really do not mind pig sties, chicken coops, not even shoveling cow dung into manure spreaders, as I once did on my uncle's midwestern farm. I do like baby chicks, ducklings, calves, lambs, and even an occasional hound. I can well enough understand the Parable of the Lost Sheep. And I am glad one of the Lord's Messianic Titles is that of the Good Shepherd. Also, I like tropical fish aquariums, all lit up in a dark room, bubbling madly, green, rocky, transparent. I like them, that is, provided I do not have to clean them. Feeding pigeons in piazzas is all right for those willing to accept the odds that they will not also be on target. I could never shoot a horse through the head with a rifle after it broke its leg, as my uncle on the farm did. Even at the time, I sensed this meant that he knew about animals and cared for them, while I did not. I was only worried about my feelings, not the horse's. To be sure, since then, my brother has endeavored valiantly to teach me something of the lore of horse flesh. But, alas, my daily doubles never come in, and neither do his.

Probably it is not wholly wrong to project human norms on the animals—"Thou Shalt Not Kill"—even Isaiah does this when he says, "He who slaughters an ox is like him who kills a man. . . ." Yet, there are considerable dangers too—I shall come back to Calcutta—in such projections. The anti-vivisectionists and the Society for the Prevention of Cruelty to Animals constantly stand on the verge of inhumanity, even though they have a point. We are not, as *Genesis* implied, to prefer animals to men, even if we do name them. They are for our use and enjoyment and life. There are, for example, more horses in America today than at any time in our history, very few of which are for food or work, though quite a few end up as meat. When I lived in Ghent in Belgium, the Sunday night special was sliced horse meat, which I ate with gusto until I found out what it was.

Animals are good in themselves, fascinating in their variety, breeds, and habits. But in a crunch, anyone who sacrifices man to animals, however this be done, is idolatrous. Thus, I am spiritually far closer to the Hindu respect for all life than I am to the Christian or liberal who approves, say, abortion or compulsory euthanasia, while joining the Sierra Club to preserve mountain goats, condors, and redwoods. I am in this also much closer to classical Marxism which was very dogmatic about what this planet was for, namely, men.

The Old Testament bloody sacrifices, as well as those of the other ancient religions—Tacitus tells us Roman augurs killed chickens before battle to read their entrails for signs of approval or disapproval—thus destroyed animals, perfect, unblemished lambs and bullocks as a sign of the Lord's total domination over his creation and our recognition of it. It is, indeed, interesting to speculate why the current orthodox Israeli have not rebuilt the Temple in Jerusalem and reinaugurated the sacrifices of the Old Law. Thus, when we remember Abraham and Christ, the problems of man, animals, and God become ever more profound. The contemporary concern we are witnessing in our sophisticated world for animal welfare and suffering—I am not referring to the price of beef and pork here—is not, I think, without its serious import. James Fallows in a recent essay in *The Atlantic* called animal liberation the "radical chic" of 1976. None the less, I sometimes suspect that we are watching nothing less than the overturn of the place of man in nature. Peter Singer extends the questions of the rights of liberty and life to animals. Using the criterion of similarity of awareness and sense perceptiveness, he believes that we must begin to consider the way we make animals suffer, the way we use them (Cf. *Moral Rights and Human Obligations*). We can no longer merely laugh off as absurd those parts of Scripture that saw the worship of animals and nature as the greatest enemy to the Lord. Men can still set up alien gods, though should they do so, the problem will still be theirs, not the animals.

In any case, my instincts are clear enough. This is why I have great sympathy for my then teen-aged nephew when he moved to Santa Barbara, of whom my sister wrote:

I must say, he and Angela (his younger, more liberated sister) are getting along much better. They take the dog (one "Corky," alas also one of that breed of enthusiastic leapers who wait expectantly by front doors) up into the hills to catch lizards, tarantulas, *etc.* You see, he needs *her* to do the actual catching 'cause he's chicken. . . .

So most of what I have to say here may justly in my case be attributed to the genes, except for that niece who cagily entraps assorted lizards, tarantulas, and so on. But, as I have suggested already, this whole subject has of late become something of a sign of contemporary moral contradiction. We do well to think about it more explicitly.

The symbols of this confusion abound. "The bird and animal programs on TV are replete with animals who never eat one another nor perform necessary functions," I once mused to a friend before the screen. "Neither do humans on TV," he dryly retorted to the destruction of my logic. Or take the advertisements for oil or timber companies. They want to keep our "trust" we are told because while drilling oil wells in the Gulf (Mexican or Persian), they are making it a place safe for those assorted little fishies shown subsequently on the screen happily nosing about a big rig sunk into the water. No squid are shown. The timber company, meanwhile, tells us its main concern is ours, the great American public, that is, turning oodles of soft possum, bevies of quail, husks of hares, and wings of plovers loose into its reforested lands. "Why not rattlesnakes?" I inquire of my fellow TV gazer. I am still not convinced, frankly, that it was not more healthy when the oil companies were adding boron and the paper companies praising Northern Tissue. We are beginning to applaud our economy for not doing anything. And Norman Macrae maintains rightly that this attitude is the one sure way that the people of the world will be most hurt ("America's Third Century." *The Economist*). Yet, my one prayer remains. When Right Guard comes up with a deodorant for cats and parakeets, I hope Joe Namath sticks to advertising pop corn poppers.

Sometimes our values are so confused. We feed our pet animals in the United States better meat and diet than a large percentage of the world's population receives. And we are not the only guilty ones here. Indeed, several years ago, the *Wall Street Journal* carried a series of articles on the aged in the United States. The surveyors were astounded to find that many elderly people eat dog food because it is nutritious and relatively cheap. We find too that so many people have unusual and foreign pets that they are escaping and multiplying and changing the local balances of nature.

I was in New Zealand not so long ago. Historically, in those Islands only wingless birds existed because they had no natural predators. This lack seems to have been due to certain deficiencies in the soil. When rabbit and deer were introduced, along with farm animals, they became pests—by human standards. So these animals had to be severely controlled. Some stories even tell of romantics who wanted to introduce the lion and tiger into those green islands. Their famous rainbow and brown trout were imported into New Zealand streams.

So this is the first thing I should like to insist upon in the context of animal liberation: The right relation between man and beast cannot be one that is based upon the questioning of the primacy of man in nature. We may well need to change our relation to the animals. But the reason for this is not that we cannot find a difference between animals and men. The balanced diet of our pets—the animal liberationists feel having a pet is itself cruel—is not more important than that of our old or that of people in other lands. My point here is *not* that I think that the reason why the old or the hungrier peoples are in the state they are is *because* we feed our pets good meat. Indeed, Herman Kahn rightly suggests that it is because we raise great amounts of grain for animals and pets that the world has a constant reserve for times of crisis (*The Next 200 Years*). More and more, there is room for both men and animals in a balanced system. Thus, the whole world will be soon enough exactly like New Zealand deciding what and how many animals it desires. But it is about the human condition that any such decision should be made, with recognition of the real value and worth of animals for what it is. From now on, wilderness is a myth. There are only greater and smaller parks, refuges, and farms.

A couple of years ago, an old friend called inviting me to dinner and to a lecture in the Masonic Auditorium on Nob Hill in San Francisco by Mr. Gerrard Durrell. "Who is Gerrard Durrell?" I ignorantly inquired. "Oh, you don't know? He writes good books about zoos and animals. Our youngest daughter has read them all and insists on hearing him." And the lecture was interesting. I again have to be grateful to the enthusiasms of my young friends. The burden of Durrell's rather short talk and film was to present the case for his zoo on the Isle of Jersey in the English Channel. Durrell is concerned especially with preserving species that are supposedly endangered. In his zoo, the endangered ones are marked by a symbolic dodo bird on the cage, a bird the Portuguese evidently once thoughtlessly wiped out. The zoo then specializes in breeding and fostering these animals and birds. In itself, this is a worthy enough project, and I have no particular quarrel with it.

However, I have plenty of reservations. Mr. Durrell's main argument for his effort was this: If we spend so much money and energy in preserving, say, a Rembrandt, we should also do the same to preserve an endangered species of animal, which after all is God's work of art. The clinching argument was always a form of "Once gone, gone for ever." The Jersey Wildlife Trust, then, strives to learn all the characteristics and habits of threatened species. It tries to reproduce them at sufficiently high levels to distribute a stock throughout the world so that the species will be assured of survival. The culprit in all of this is, not surprisingly, something called man, or sometimes, modern civilization. What is of interest in all this is what is left unspoken. We know perfectly well, for example, that before man ever appeared on Earth, myriads of species disappeared from the earth, never to return. Just how absolute, in other words, is this evidently self-evident law that no species must ever be allowed to disappear? At what cost do we save them? If we save them, are we preventing some further modification?

Furthermore, we used to believe, if we were avant-garde, in a thing called evolution, commonly defined as the survival of the fittest by a well-known 19th century author in a ship called, of all things, the *Beagle*. Presently, apparently, we are being told somewhat indirectly that evolution is bad *if* some species does not survive. Yet, as Eugene Rabinowitch remarked, the only animals whose disappearance would really jeopardize man's life on earth would be the bacteria in his body (*The Times*. London, 19 Ap. '72). And J. R. Harlan observed in the *Scientific American* that the number of animal species we really depend upon is very few and these are now totally dependent on man for their survival. "Although man must care for his domesticates," he concluded, "the human population of the world eats or starves according to the performance of those few plants and animals that nourish man." ("The Plants and Animals That Nourish Man.") In the older evolutionary theory, if I recall correctly, eventually nothing survived except the fittest, which always, by definition, was something new. The death of the last passenger pigeon in the zoo in, I believe, Philadelphia, however, now becomes something of a modern tragedy almost at the level of *King Lear*. If God created all the animals (and presumably, bugs and toads) in nature, it is a big corporate sin, an old theological idea that keeps coming back in different forms, to allow anything to disappear. Consequently, we spend money and talent for this purpose. Even though there is beginning a reaction to zoos as unnatural, these are still good days for owning a zoo.

In all of this, I believe, a rather striking contradiction exists. On the one hand, we are told that the survival of animals is up to us, presumably the fittest by the oldest definition or we would not still be about. On the other hand, it is intimated that the preservation of animals and plants and termites really conditions our survival so that we cannot do too much with the Earth for our own welfare because it is too fragile. One really must wonder in what sense we can really speak of evolution anymore. Evolution itself strikes me sometimes as itself an endangered species. Linguists, for example, are quite certain that language did not evolve. In any case, either nature is still evolving—who could have ever turned her off?—in which case we should not worry because what does not survive, for whatever reason, is simply unfit; or else man is now completely in charge of nature, in which case it is up to man's rational planning, not evolution, to define what and how many animals and bugs and plants like poison ivy and roses and dandelions should survive. In other words, everything is now a zoo, or a Chinese garden, or a farm, or a playing field. This is why Durrell was forced to make his most telling argument for the preservation of rare animal species through an analogy with art, something that is beyond use categories.

With a niece and nephew, I was once invited to attend a double feature—*Jesus Christ Superstar* and *Bless the Beasts and Children. Jesus Christ Superstar,* of course, amidst rather good music, could not figure out who he was, God, man, or both. In the second film, the beasts and the children—both of whom The-Lord-Who-Figured-Out-Who-He-Was blessed— were in a similar predicament. Penned buffalo were shot for sport by rather grim hunters with high powered rifles in the movie. A group of children were appalled by this. They believed these buffalo were free spirits and needed liberation.

The humans who shot them were pictured as beasts. All of this is especially curious if we can recall Aristotle's remark in *The Politics* where he said that someone who does not naturally live in the *Polis,* in the city, is either a beast or a god. Evidently today, the divisions in the great chain of being have never been more obscure. I see few more graphic signs of a profound confusion among us than when a Jesus Christ Superstar cannot figure out where he belongs in the chain of being, while children see buffalo to be better than men. In this connection, James Fellows reported:

> Last year . . . the New York *Times* reported that high school students in the area were sabotaging their biology labs; one fifteen-year-old girl from Westchester County rescued "the rat on the bad diet" from a classroom nutrition experiment and nursed it back to health at home. . . . "Their view of life," (a teacher reported) "is so much broader than mine. They don't want life washed away, whether it's dog or an elephant or an amoeba. That to me is fantastic." [See p 73 in this volume.]

Thus, Gods, men, animals, bugs, plants, and amoeba are all mixed up. And if we recall biological engineering and the DNR, we feel we are soon to break the link between inanimate nature and life. Everything is everything else—the great project of the medieval alchemist has almost succeeded.

This brings me back to Calcutta. A couple of years ago, I spent some days there. Just like every other westerner who has ever been in that city, I was appalled by the emaciated cows wandering all about the city. If there is ever a place that needs the meditation of *Genesis,* it is Calcutta. Yet, as I walked those streets, joyous because of the military victory over Pakistan in Bangladesh, streets that so shock one that he is hardly able to see what is there, I began to wonder if the Christian's notion of man's place in creation will not eventually make the Hindu notion of reverence for all life possible, indeed practical. The paradox of the most affluent society killing untold fetuses while spending enormous sums on pet food and zoos, alongside the Hindu society needing more food but letting cattle and monkeys roam where they might seemed too startling. Added to this is the fact, as Herman

Kahn also indicated, that India is in fact a very rich country in terms of resources and agricultural potential, that its problems are its own political choices and attitudes (*The Next 200 Years*).

In such light, surely something like the Eighth Psalm means more than we traditionally give it credit for:

> Yet thou hast made him a little less than God.
> and dost crown him with glory and honor.
> Thou hast given him dominion over the works of thy hands;
> thou hast put all things under his feet,
> all sheep and oxen, and also the beasts of the field,
> the birds of the air, and the fish of the sea,
> whatever passes along the paths of the sea.

Some day, it strikes me, we shall all be vegetarian, if not "mineralitarian"—that is, people whose food is largely created directly from component parts without passing through the animal cycle or even the vegetable cycle (Cf. A. McPherson, "Synthetic Food for Tomorrow's Billions," *Beyond Left and Right*). I believe the animal cycle is for our use in our present state of "evolution." But it will pass away. The free market and human inventiveness will and is producing foods of soybean and other plants that are equal to or surpass those meat foods inefficiently produced by animals (Cf. Jean Mayer, "The Dimensions of Human Hunger," *The Scientific American*). We forget that practically all the animal flesh we eat comes from animals largely "created" in our agricultural colleges and corporate laboratories. Someday, there will be a Society for the Preservation of the Aberdeen Angus, the Suffolk Sheep, the Poland China Hog, the Plymouth Rock Chicken, and the Silver Martin Rabbit, an animal whose very existence I discovered for the first time at the Santa Clara County Fair, in a cage, beautiful animal. Furthermore, there will be myriads of animals and birds (and insects) we do not yet possess. They will all be mostly (God forbid!) pets, in houses, zoos, and larger parks euphemistically called wildernesses, all well attended by expensive experts from the Oklahoma Aggies or Cal Davis or Iowa State, places designed for us to walk through and look about.

C. S. Lewis used to ask (I believe in the *Four Loves*) about the friendship or love of animals. His point was a good one. The more we are with an animal—Mr. Durrell described the various animals he has had to sleep with to keep them warm in a strange environment—the more we individualize it by our care, the less it is "animal." The apocalyptic end of *Isaiah*, so many times painted by the medievals and by the American primitive painter Edward Hicks, says:

> The wolf and the lamb shall feed together,
> the lion shall eat straw like the ox;
> and dust shall be the serpents food,
> They shall not hurt or destroy in all my holy mountain,
> says the Lord.

Many such things, of course, already happen in Fleishhacker Zoo down off Ocean Beach. The peace of animals depends, as Thomas Aquinas held, upon the condition and care of men, their reverence for life, their technology, their sense of priorities. Animals are to be loved. Their preservation is not unlike a museum that preserves an El Greco.

Yet, our hierarchy of values must be clear. And more especially the reasons for it. One human baby is worth the whole of the animal kingdom, even though the same baby delights in chicks and ducks and geese and, yes, hound dogs. We must not continue to create a modern Moloch in which we sacrifice babies to Baal or biology—neither babies nor full human lives in areas less fortunate than our own. It is all right to sacrifice animals to the Lord and to our needs—even though the day is probably fast coming when, as in our faith, the bloody victim will be replaced by an unbloody one, when we will realize the progress only in retrospect, when we will insist on living quite healthily without eating animals, as most nutritionists insist that we can do.

In the Fifth Book of the *Histories* of Tacitus, he recounts the Roman version of the Capture of Jerusalem, though we lack his actual account of the Destruction of the Temple under Titus in 70 AD.

> Moyses . . . gave them a novel form of worship, opposed to all that is practised by other men. Things sacred with us, with them have no sanctity, while they allow what with us is forbidden. . . .

They slay the ram, seemingly in derision of Hammon, and they sacrifice the ox, because the Egyptians worship it as Apis. . . .

Prodigies had occurred, which this nation, prone to superstition, but hating all religious rites, did not deem it lawful to expiate by offering and sacrifice. There had been seen hosts joining battle in the skies, the fiery gleem of arms, the temple illuminated by a sudden radiance from the clouds.

The doors of the inner shrine were suddenly thrown open, and a voice of more than mortal tone was heard to cry that the Gods were departing. At the same instant, there was a mighty stir as of departure. Some few put a fearful meaning on these events, but in most there was a firm persuasion, that in the ancient records of their priests there was contained a prediction of how at this very time the East was to grow powerful, and rulers, coming from Judea, were to acquire universal empire.

For Tacitus, of course, these universal rulers were Vespasian and Titus. Matthew, using a very similar description of the scene on Golgotha, believed it was Someone Else. Titus then destroyed the place of bloody sacrifice, while Matthew cited a Roman centurion—"And behold, the curtain of the Temple was torn in two. . . ."—as saying, "This surely was the Son of God." Gods and men, animals, plants, and minerals. . . . The destiny of the Earth is for it to be a garden within the City of God in which we are to walk in the cool of the evening and converse with the Lord midst his creatures.

The New Zealand poet, James K. Baxter, wrote:

Brief is the visiting angel. In the corridors of hunger
Our lives entwined suffer the common ill:
Living and dying, breathing and begetting.
Meanwhile on maimed gravestones under towering fennel
Moves the bright lizard, sunloved, basking in
The moment of animal joy.
          ["Elegy at the Year's End," *The Rock Woman.*]

When the animals no longer suffer—the lion shall eat straw like the ox—it means that the natural cycle of eating and being eaten will cease. The beasts shall be cared for. But while the suffering of animals can and should be transformed (we do need to care for their lives), we humans, none the less, shall still know suffering. For our lot and theirs is not ultimately identical.

Some doubt God because we—his creatures—are not all the same. There are those who think that Fido and the buffalos and the earthworm, which Albert Schweitzer put back into the ground, should share our immortality. And for too many, Belsen and the abortion clinics and the poor in Calcutta are of less significance than the death of the last Passenger Pigeon in Philadelphia in 1910, or wherever. But it is not so. Indeed, to make it so is still idolatry, sacrificing to Moloch. The ancient sins are still our own.

Yet, pets are pets, and we should care for them—for this is what their destiny is to be. We shall need many of them for a long while, to be sure, for food, for learning. But still the animals are companions of a sort, co-dwellers in this niche of space we paradoxically call home. The Twenty-first *Fioretto* continues:

And St Francis went and made nests for all (the turtle-doves); and they took their nests, and began to lay eggs, and hatched them without fear before the eyes of the brothers; and they were as tame and as familiar with St Francis and all the other brothers as if they had been domestic fowls always accustomed to be fed by them; and they would not depart until St Francis with his blessing gave them leave to go. . . .

The *Fioretti* of St. Francis are not inspired. Yet, especially today, I sometimes wonder about these legends. St. Francis was, however, a Christian. For him the animals always led to God. They too somehow asked for his blessing.

Anyone who hates dogs and children cannot be all bad. Bless the Beasts and Children. Thou hast given him dominion over the works of thy hands. Animals too suffer. Brief is the visiting angel. Prodigies abound which this nation did not deem it expedient to expiate by offering and sacrifice. Love Me, Love my Dog. "Look at the birds of the air: they neither sow nor reap nor gather into barns, and yet your heavenly Father feeds them. Are you not of more value then they?" We learn to love animals as Christians. You, mortal men, are of more value than they—and yet, they are beautiful, even the ladybugs, lizards, tarantulas, caterpillars, as well as the cutthroat trout of Lake Pend d'Oreille, the Aberdeen Angus Bull, the mountain goat, and the swallow, which goes back to

Capistrano, to a place in which the Brothers of Francis in 1776 built a mission on the shores of the vast Pacific.

Nevertheless, if we are to be friends: *Contain Your Dog.*

Something of the Law and the Prophets is surely contained in this one saying.

II. ANIMAL RIGHTS: HISTORY, PHILOSOPHY, OPINION

EDITOR'S INTRODUCTION

During the past ten years professional philosophers, theologians, conservationists, and biologists, among others, have given a great deal of serious consideration to our moral responsibility toward other living creatures. This section examines the question of animal rights versus human needs.

In the first selection, Richard Adams, author of *Watership Down* and *The Plague Dogs*, argues that humans should develop a sense of respect and justice toward animals, treating them as living creatures rather than as objects or toys. Next, James Fallows, writing in the *Atlantic Monthly*, continues Adams's theme by pointing out how in the past animals have been used and abused, even wasted, and how the animal rights movement is pressing for moderation and improvement in the area of animal welfare, particularly in laboratory research.

The third article, by Nicholas Wade, writing in *Science*, describes the extraordinary public reaction to the news that the American Museum of Natural History had conducted sensory-deprivation experiments on cats. The next three selections—all letters to the editor of *Science* in response to the Wade article—provide examples of just how complex and partisan the issue of vivisection can be.

In the seventh article, again from *Science*, Constance Holden adds her voice to the concern about abuses on factory farms and pleads for more humane practices and less scientific means in raising animals for food.

THE UNEASY ENTENTE[1]

When the Lord had created Adam and placed him in the Garden of Eden, he charged Adam with naming all the animals. This myth makes clear that from the outset God regarded human beings as having a responsibility to know about and be able to recognize the animals. What meaning are we to draw from this story for our own situation in the world today?

Few of us in England or the United States, except possibly children, find ourselves frequently called upon to combat actual cruelty to animals. We sometimes come across individual instances of negligence or thoughtlessness, but the kind of thing that was thought legitimate amusement in the sixteenth century (e.g., a clothed ape tied to the back of a pony and set upon by dogs) has, fortunately, vanished much as slavery has vanished. But just think about this. The British Cruelty to Animals Act was passed in 1876. In 1878 the total number of licensed experiments performed on living animals in Britain was 270. In 1970 the total was 5,580,876. More than 4.5 million of these were done without anesthetics. In 1876 there were 23 persons licensed under the act to perform experiments; in 1972, 16,143.

How many of the experiments were necessary? A large number are undoubtedly justified. Since 1876, medical and veterinary research has advanced by quantum leaps. Many new subjects of study have emerged—chemotherapy, virology, endocrinology, radiobiology, et cetera—and we have come to see disease as a disorder of function rather than a product of causes alien to the body. But what are we to think of the commercial experiments—the forcible feeding of a new lipstick or shaving soap to groups of animals until 50 percent of them are dead; the squirting of a new hair spray

[1] Article entitled "People and Animals: the Uneasy Entente" by Richard Adams, author of *Watership Down. Harper's.* 252:3. Mr. '76. Reprinted by permission of Harold Ober Associates. Copyright © 1976 by Harper's Magazine.

into rabbits' eyes until they are blind; or compelling dogs to smoke thirty cigarettes a day and killing them after months or years to find out how we ourselves can best indulge in this vice? No one thinks the scientists are sadistic maniacs, but I wonder how many people have really considered what is involved, especially in "psychological" experiments involving "punishment." Everyone should read Peter Singer's book, *Animal Liberation,* and consider for himself such questions as how much avoidable suffering is involved in slaughtering. Animals have no attorneys, and their only rights are the ones we confer upon them.

I am not advocating sentimentality, just the reverse. There is far too much sentimentality toward animals in modern culture. . . . Everyone must think out what he believes to be the ethics of this subject. I have no blueprint or solution to advance. I say only that we should not *waste* the animals.

As always true knowledge breeds true respect. If we really knew more about all animals, justice would follow. . . .

That's what we need. We're *responsible* for the animals as part of the beauty of the world. What exactly does that involve? . . .

WHAT DID NOAH SAVE THEM FOR?[2]

For many years, I have held what I like to think of as the good-hearted carnivore's view toward our fellow members of the animal kingdom. It consists of great tenderness toward individual animals, combined with a certain ruthlessness about the larger purposes that other species may be called upon to serve. No creatures have ever received more love, attention, or general good treatment than the steer, chickens, pigeons, and goat I raised as a child—not to mention the usual cats, dogs, hamsters, and fish. In the back of my mind, I knew that

[2] Article entitled "Lo the Poor Animals! What Did Noah Save Them For?" by James Fallows, freelance journalist. *Atlantic Monthly.* 238:58–65. S. '76. Copyright © 1976, by the Atlantic Monthly Company, Boston, Mass. Reprinted with permission.

a dark fate awaited my beloved Angus calf, but that did not keep me from brushing the tangles out of his long black hair or worrying when the flies got to him.

I never dreamed of hunting, and the sight of a four-inch perch flopping desperately on the riverbank put me off fishing for years. On Boy Scout trips we would lurk late into the night in the hope of glimpsing our friend the raccoon. En route to the Reptiles merit badge, I put up with an instructor who said that the way to deal with nonpoisonous snakes, when they were being captured for study, was to hold them by the tail and let them bite your hand until they wearied, a process that took several minutes the one time I saw it demonstrated.

When these labors of Assisi were completed, I would dig happily into a nice hamburger or a thick, juicy steak. I never ate my own animals, of course; within 4-H circles it was an acceptable deviation, a perfectly manly form of squeamishness, to wish to sell the animals you had raised rather than eat the flanks you had so often patted. But when someone else's pet was on the plate, I had no such hesitation. For this, after all, was the way of the world. Walt Disney's nature films offered proof to anyone who might doubt. There, on the living desert, snakes devoured baby birds, coyotes ate jackrabbits. Under the sea, starfish ate oysters, big fish ate little fish, sharks ate their wounded brethren. In the world at large, it seemed, any creature was perfectly willing to eat any other it could reach its jaws around, so why shouldn't we?

Sometimes the natural processes were so cruel and horrible as to make animal husbandry seem positively beatific by comparison. The day I learned about evil was when I walked out to feed my flock of pigeons and discovered them, every one, murdered by a ferret that had not even bothered to dine. He had simply beheaded them, spattering blood over their brown and white feathers, and left them in the sawdust on the floor. This, I realized, demonstrated the nobility and the tragedy of man. Nobility, because unlike the ferret we ate what we killed. Tragedy, because unlike any other animal we could feel pity for the creatures on which we fed.

Given the widespread popularity of pets, the general re-
vulsion against outright cruelty, and the relative scarcity of
vegetarians, I have always assumed that most people feel the
same way. But recently there have been signs that this carefully balanced philosophy will no longer do. It is not just the
environmentalists who have been speaking up, with their
warnings that the wild kingdom is in peril, but a new and
more vociferous movement, asserting that all animals, even
the most abundant and least charming of them, have been denied their rights to health and happiness by an inconsiderate
human race.

Last year, for example, the New York *Times* reported that
high school students in the area were sabotaging their biology
labs; one fifteen-year-old girl from Westchester County res-
cued "the rat on the bad diet" from a classroom nutrition experiment and nursed it back to health at home. In Merion
Station, Pennsylvania, students at the Akiba Hebrew Academy carefully returned amoebae and paramecia to their petri
dish when one experiment was over, rather than flush them
down the sink, "It didn't matter to me that the life of these
creatures was going down the drain," said Dr. Leonard
Krause, their teacher, "but it did to these kids. Their view of
life is so much broader than mine. They don't want life
washed away, whether it's a dog or an elephant or an amoeba.
That to me is fantastic."

Even in the wilds of Texas, where ranchers still nail dead
coyotes and chicken hawks to their fence posts as a taunt to
wild predators in general, times seem to have changed. The
two small Texas towns of Noack and Lometa held their rattle-
snake roundups this spring, as they have done every spring for
years. Thousands of the creatures were captured, exhibited,
beheaded, and fried. But this year, in addition to the partici-
pants, there was also a group of dissenters who made the in-
disputable point that the hunt was hard on the snakes. "There
are a growing number of people," one member of this group
wrote in the Austin *American-Statesman*, "who recognize
speciesism as the bigotry that it is. Mistreatment of any animal, human or nonhuman, is wrong." A few weeks later, Aus-

tin's Armadillo World Headquarters, the country-music palace that had been second only to the Astrodome as an outlet for Lone Star Beer, cut off its Lone Star contract because the company persisted in sponsoring live armadillo races. "The only way to protect an armadillo," said Eddie Wilson, the Armadillo's manager, "is to leave it alone, rather than rounding them up and capturing them."

Advertisements depicting an agonized raccoon, its foot caught in a steel leg-hold trap, have become a frequent sight in the newspapers, placed there by groups campaigning to have the traps outlawed. Zoo directors in many cities, who were just learning how to thwart vandals who stick tennis balls down the throats of hippopotamuses or slay baby rabbits in the children's zoos, have suddenly been assailed by those who claim to love animals better than they. "Zoos should be phased out," says Alice Herrington of a New York-based organization called Friends of Animals, Inc. "I don't think man can justify this form of exploitation of animals." Using dark images of the concentration camps, another of the animals' rights groups, United Action for Animals, warns that zoos are the scene of sinister scientific experiments upon the captive herds.

Such traditional friends of the animal as the Humane Society and the Society for the Prevention of Cruelty to Animals (SPCA) have lately come in for flank attacks from the more militant groups. The Humane Society is condemned for acquiescing in the system of laboratory experiments that kill millions of animals each year. Recently, for example, the society made the mistake of proposing a set of "Guiding Principles" for the use of animals in high school experiments. United Action for Animals, always quick on the trigger, responded with a blast: "What difference does it *really* make whether the student himself kills animals 'humanely' or whether he watches someone else do it? It's the contempt for life—the killing itself—that is at issue."

The SPCA has become a victim of numbers. Some 72,000 cats and dogs, the great majority of them unwanted, are born in this country *every day*. Some join wild animal packs—New

York, Los Angeles, Chicago, and other large cities are estimated to contain at least 100,000 wild dogs each—but most of them end up in animal shelters, where the city humane departments and the SPCA must finally put them to death. The society has tested a variety of machines to make the killings painless, but the more militant animal groups criticize it for doing this dirty job at all.

During the last session of Congress, sixty-three representatives cosponsored a bill offered by Edward Koch of Manhattan to create a Commission on Humane Treatment of Animals which would set standards for farms, laboratories, and fur trappers in the wild. "The subject of animal welfare gets more mail throughout the year than any other issue," Koch said in introducing the bill. "Not only in my office, but in almost every congressional office in the country." In May, Federal Judge Charles Richey threw the tuna industry into panic when he ruled that fishermen would have to abandon the modern equivalent of shooting fish in a barrel—tracking schools of tuna down by sonar, and then scooping them up in gigantic nets—because tens of thousands of porpoises were killed each year in the process. The fishing lobby appealed the decision, most naturalists rejoiced, but one contingent of hard-line vegetarians said that the "victory" was irrelevant, since the tuna were still being oppressed.

It is words like "oppressed" that provide the key to much of the new animals' rights movement. Dignified old humane societies have been around for years, but today's "animal liberation" forces have the same relation to them as the Black Panthers had to George Washington Carver. Indeed, with the waning of the competition, the animal cause is already a cinch winner of the Radical Chic award for 1976. No one cares about the Indians anymore; the whites of Westchester County are no longer trooping down to Harlem to paint front stoops on Saturday afternoon. Wonder of wonders, a trace of humor seems to have reappeared in relations between the sexes. But no such note of moderation is yet admissible to the canon of animal liberation. For the moment, the forces are in strident upswing, riding an undeniably powerful issue which

they have encrusted with much no-compromise rhetoric.
What Ralph Nader felt about the Corvair, what Susan
Brownmiller felt about men rings out from passages like this
about the enemies of animals:

> This book is about the tyranny of human over nonhuman ani-
> mals. This tyranny has caused and today is still causing an amount
> of pain and suffering that can only be compared to that which re-
> sulted from the centuries of tyranny by white humans over black
> humans. The struggle against this tyranny is a struggle as impor-
> tant as any of the moral and social issues that have been fought
> over in recent years.

There are the opening words of *Animal Liberation,* a book
by an Australian philosopher named Peter Singer, which . . .
since its publication has become both the clearest symptom
and the most fully articulated manifesto of the animal movement. Along with providing a good deal of powerful exposé
about mistreatment of animals in laboratories and on the
farm, the book has two qualities that distinguish it, and the
movement, from the animal-lovers of old. The first is a philosophy which is far more "radical" than simple tender-hearted-
ness toward cats and dogs. Roughly speaking, Singer argues
that men have no right to "discriminate" against animals (by
killing them, using them in unnecessary experiments, dissect-
ing them in labs, etc.) because nearly all of them can feel
pain, and many are more intelligent than a retarded or coma-
tose human being. We don't kill a retarded child, Singer says:
we don't dissect people with brain damage—and therefore, to
treat an animal any differently is to discriminate on "species-
ist" grounds.

Second, the book demonstrates quite nicely how this
year's oppressed group is part of a great chain of being,
stretching back to oppressed groups of years gone by.

The title of the book's first chapter is more or less a call to
battle for those who have fought the good fight before. "All
Animals Are Equal, or why supporters of liberation for Blacks
and Women should support Animal Liberation too." Numerous other sections of the book are devoted to the hair-splitting
work of defining a proper attitude toward animals—an effort
so very reminiscent of the burning issues of the past. Should

we invite a black family to dinner? Should we resist the draft? Should we take our tin cans to the recycling center? Should we eat a clam? "Those who want to be absolutely certain that they are not causing suffering will not eat mollusks either, but somewhere between a shrimp and an oyster seems as good a place to draw the line as any, and better than most."

The ancestral source of tension between men and beasts—the fact that we eat them—is, of course, one of the issues in the animal renaissance; the question of becoming a vegetarian is often in the air. But the ancestral event, the slaughter itself, is not the focus of concern. The march toward technology, which has come so often at the expense of the peace of mind of men and animals alike, has, in at least a few places, taken some of the gore and terror out of putting beasts to death.

One of those places is the Iowa Beef Processors installation in Amarillo, Texas, the largest slaughterhouse in the world and one of the most modern. Three thousand cattle are trucked in each morning from farms and feedlots on the surrounding flatlands; by the end of the day, all of them are dead. In the slaughterhouses of old, there were two terrible moments of brutal, panicked struggle. The first was when the cattle smelled blood in the air and screamed and lurched in their desperate attempts to avoid the knocking box; the second, when the man with the poleax swung down on the broad skulls, sending blood spurting when he hit and crushing noses or eyes when he missed the dead-center target. Aficionados of bullfights might have liked it, for the animals went down fighting, but it revealed a little too clearly the violence on which our comforts were based.

At modern slaughterhouses, like the one in Amarillo, the desperate struggles have been replaced by an eerily tranquil march toward death. The difference arose from application of a central principle of animal locomotion. "Cattle hate to go around a corner," says Glen Hoaglund, the engineer who designed the Iowa Beef facility, "but they'll go around a curved surface with hardly any problem." Iowa Beef has designed its plant to give the cows as many of these curves as possible; from the time they step off the truck until the moment they

are stunned for the kill, the cattle follow a virtually continuous curving path, like the interior of the Guggenheim Museum. Cowboys lean on the sides of the chutes, electric cattle
prods in their hands, but most of the cattle trudge on placidly.

In one day at the plant I heard almost none of the terrified
bellows which used to rise continually from the older abattoirs. At the end of their trudge, the cattle were stunned by a
young man whose long blond hair hung out below his hard
hat and who wore a turquoise ornament at his neck. Using a
"captive bolt" stunner—a metal cylinder the size of an elon-
gated Coke can which drives a steel shaft the size of a ciga-
rette into the animal's brain—he rendered cattle unconscious
at the rate of six or eight a minute, leaving a small round hole
in the center of their foreheads. Seconds later, the unconscious animals were hoisted up by a hind leg, slit across the
throat, and drained of their blood.

By no one's standards was this a pleasant scene; the very
calmness of the doomed cattle was as redolent of the concentration camps as the older abattoirs were of primeval battles.
And, as the cattle were dismantled, all their gleaming viscera
and brains exposed, one could not help but marvel at the
complexity and delicacy of these beings whose lives were
being extinguished in such numbers. It was sobering, but it
did not seem cruel.

Many of the older slaughterhouses still exist; about 20
percent of the cattle killed each year are killed in small, anti-
quated abattoirs, where the man with the poleax still does his
work. Another 8 percent are slaughtered—delicate issue—
according to kosher laws, which require that the animal be
conscious at the moment its throat is slit. In a kosher abattoir,
live, terrified cattle are suspended by the hind leg, their hip
joints often rupturing, and left to hang until killed. "Whenever you take an animal's life, it's a terrible thing," said one of
the officials at Iowa Beef. "You can't feel very happy in any of
these places. But this is sure better than a kosher slaughterhouse. To me, *that* is cruelty."

Demand for kosher meat has soared recently—it has risen
by more than 30 percent in the last five years, mainly because

of a growing reputation among non-Jews as a high-quality item—but the new animal movement has spent little time on kosher slaughter. It has concentrated instead on what happens to the animals before they reach the abattoir. Their target is "factory farming," the system of raising animals in extremely close confinement. In the United States, the poultry business represents factory farming in its most advanced state. Many chickens now spend their entire lives in indoor batteries, scores of thousands of them under one roof. Typically, five adult birds share less than 400 square inches of floor space—about the size of a newspaper's front page. The chickens dislike this enough that they must be routinely "debeaked"; if their beaks are not removed, they will tear each other apart.

Somewhat more ghoulish is the factory farm approach to raising veal. Years ago, "veal" meant the flesh of calves, usually male dairy cattle, that were killed quite soon after birth. Having eaten no food but their mothers' milk, the calves had flesh that was soft, pink, and pale. But the calves were small, and inefficient as sources of meat. To increase their yields, farmers began sustaining the calves in a condition of unnaturally prolonged infancy. Most veal calves are still slaughtered within a week of their birth, but the highest-quality meat comes from calves who are taken from their mothers and penned up in small cages, too short to allow them to turn around. There they are fed a diet full of everything except iron, which would turn their flesh a rich, hemoglobin-filled red.

"The anemic calf's insatiable craving for iron," Peter Singer says, "is one of the reasons why the producer is anxious to prevent it from turning around in its stall. Although calves, like pigs, normally prefer not to go near their own urine or manure, urine does contain some iron. The desire for iron is strong enough to overcome the natural repugnance, and the anemic calves will lick the slats that are impregnated with urine."

Having grown accustomed, these last few years, to thinking of themselves as heroes in the war against starvation,

agricultural scientists do not like horror stories such as these
at all. At the more advanced institutions, they have responded as they did when heavy pesticide use fell from fashion several years ago. Go to any progressive agricultural college these days, and you will find the rising young researchers
working not on new pesticides but on insect-resistant plants
that will not need pesticides at all. Their counterparts in animal research also seem to have sensed that the tide is turning
away from some of the more brutal forms of factory farming.
"It should be easy to avoid making those calves anemic," says
Dudley Smith of the Agricultural Experiment Station at
Texas A&M, one of several scientists to suggest that research
could produce a dye that could turn normal, healthy flesh
pale without affecting its texture or flavor.

But some of the other forms of factory farming remain a
question of economic efficiency; the poultry industry estimates that battery-raised chickens, even when the losses from
cannibalism and general ill health are taken into account, are
about 20 percent cheaper to raise than those that roam free
on the range. The animals' rights forces also seem to recognize that factory farming is a question of economics, and pro-
pose to fight it on those grounds. "Unless we boycott meat,"
Peter Singer says, "we are, each one of us, contributing to the
continued existence, prosperity, and growth of factory farming and all the other cruel practices used in rearing animals
for food."

All this sounds fine, but even in their headiest moments
animal partisans must realize that the fight cannot make
much difference. Singer does couch his argument in terms of
economic impact, but the only certain effect is on personal
purity—whether we will "contribute to the continued existence" of the evil factory farms. The "we" to whom this plea
is addressed are roughly the same "we" who boycotted let-
tuce and grapes—conceivably enough people to make a dent
in the market, certainly not enough to close down the meat
industry. No more than Luddites could turn back the Industrial Revolution will Peter Singer make all of us into vegetarians. With greater or lesser degrees of confinement, with more

or less cruelty in the kill, farms and abattoirs will be with us forever. In time, the passion of the Luddites gave way to that of reformers who tried to reduce the brutality of factory life, and this in the long run may be the contribution Animal Liberation makes to the beasts we continue to consume.

But it is not in the farm or the slaughterhouse that the fiercest battles over animals' rights are really being waged. They are being fought instead in medical and scientific laboratories, where more than 200,000 animals lose their lives every day. During the course of one year, some 80 million animals under experimentation are dissected, observed, electroshocked, and killed in American laboratories: 50 million mice and rats, 20 million frogs, two million birds, half a million each of hamsters, guinea pigs, and rabbits, 200,000 dogs and turtles, and hundreds of thousands of cats, pigs, snakes, monkeys, and animals of other descriptions. To militants like Eleanor Seiling, these "death sciences" are an offense that cannot be allowed to continue.

Sixteen years ago, Miss Seiling, then a secretary for a securities firm, walked into a pet store in Manhattan and saw a tank of goldfish that were being eaten alive by fungus. "I told the store owner about it, and he wouldn't do anything at all. I couldn't get any action out of the Humane Society either. That was really the thing that started me off, made me think something more had to be done." In 1967, she quit her job and, using her own savings and the funds of her friends, established United Action for Animals. Nearly ten years later, the group has become the Nader's Raiders of the animals' rights world, feared by all they deal with, and armed with facts for battle.

The UAA's world is one which teems with enemies—its representatives describe at length the "experimental animal establishment," spiritual brother to the military–industrial complex, whose barons grow rich on the profits of death—but one of its real obstacles is the good press that the healing sciences have won. At the mere mention of medical experimentation, most thoughts turn to dedicated doctors working late in their labs, perhaps testing insulin on dogs who seem to understand the nobility of their sacrifice, or studying cancer in white mice so as to cure it in man. The only people who might object to such goings-on are the dotty old antivivisectionists.

In presenting a vastly different picture of laboratory work, the UAA has made use not only of considerable hyperbole but of a Great Truth about scientific life and a brilliant propaganda technique. The great truth, which shows some insight into organizational life, is that many experiments are performed for the same reason many graduate dissertations are written—not because anyone really wants the answers, but because grants have been awarded and research contracts let; there are appointments, promotions, advanced degrees at stake. The mechanics of the profession require that scientists experiment, and there is nothing to impede their use or misuse of the experimental animals.

Miss Seiling and her associates support their claim through the UAA's great propaganda technique—poring through scientific journals to find the experimenters' own descriptions of what they did to animals in the lab, and what they learned as a consequence. In one of its reports, the UAA provides a list, stretching back for nearly a century, of obviously painful and apparently repetitious experiments on death by overheating. In 1973, the pamphlet says,

the US government paid Israeli experimenters to run dogs to a temperature of 113 and death on a treadmill to show that heatstroke victims *should be cooled.* . . . Back in 1881, researchers electric-shocked and convulsed dogs to a temperature of 113 and death to show that overheated bodies *should be cooled.* Even Claude Bernard, the world's most famous animal experimenter, produced heat deaths in animals back in 1876.

Here is a description of one of the earlier heat experiments, conducted in 1880:

Animals exposed to natural heat in box with glass lid placed on brick pavement in hot sun.
Rabbit. Body temp. 109.5° F; Jumps, and "kicks hind legs with great fury," has convulsive attacks. 112° F, lies on side slobbering. Temp. 120° F, lies on side gasping and squealing weakly. 114.5° F, dead [body temp.].

Pigeon. Temp. inside brick box 130°. Pigeon placed inside in direct contact with hot brick. 20 minutes later pigeon unable to stand, semi-conscious, and in convulsion. Temp. 120°: Dead. Experimenter said that "his thermometer did not register higher than 120°" and that his hand "could hardly bear the heat of the pigeon's flesh."
Cat. Temp. inside box 130° F. Cat placed inside. Struggled "violently and savagely." Animal conscious, growing weaker. After a five minute convulsion, cat was plunged into cold water. Body opened. "Heart found to be still beating and distended with blood. . . ."
Rabbits and Cats. Heads fitted with double "bonnet" of india rubber or pig bladder. Brains heated by running hot water through bonnet:
Rabbit. Water temp 140° F, scalp puffy and swollen. Rapid breathing, violent struggles. Semi-conscious, but eyes sensitive to touch. Water temp. 180° F, convulsion, death. Skull opened, thermometer plunged into brain. Brain temp. 117° F. . . .
Kitten. Water temp. to head 170° F. Semi-conscious, eye pupils strongly contracted. General convulsion, beginning in jaw muscles. During convulsion, thermometer plunged into brain. Brain temp. 107.5° F.

"Oddly enough," the UAA concludes, after listing similar experiments, with similar findings, through every decade of this century, "the real maker of our Federal science policy is a man long dead. The idol of today's federal subsidy recipients, whose political pressure determines the size of the subsidy, is Claude Bernard, who lived from 1813 to 1878. . . . Bernard is remembered and revered especially for his advice to his students, 'Why think when you can experiment?' "

The UAA is easily the shrillest voice in a generally immoderate field. It has no time for halfway solutions and regularly goes hunting for congressmen such as Edward Koch or Richard Ottinger (both Democrats of New York) who make "compromise" efforts on the animals' behalf. "They're dedicated, almost fanatically, to getting rid of pain at any cost," says one congressional assistant who, having dealt with the UAA before, is not eager to be identified for the record. "We tend to feel that if there's no alternative to experimenting with animals, and if a certain experiment will help human welfare, then it should go ahead. But the UAA won't put up with that for a minute." Nonetheless, the statistics in the UAA's reports are generally acknowledged to be accurate; the arguments are about where necessity ends and excess begins. They do make at least a prima facie case that something is amiss in the lab. Some of them list painful experiments which yield rather obvious results. In the spring of 1971, researchers at Princeton starved 265 rats to death, and discovered that "under conditions of fatal thirst and starvation, young rats two to three weeks old are nearly ten times as active in spontaneous movement as normal adults given food and water." In the fall of 1972, a postdoctoral researcher at Duke removed portions of the cerebral cortex from nine shrews and then tested their ability to learn. He discovered that all of the animals with injured brains were "retarded" compared to the normal animals, and "the animal with the most retarded performance had the largest lesion, and the animal with the least retarded performance had the smallest lesion."

Cats have had their testicles crushed, to establish that this is as painful for them as it is for humans. Monkeys are driven into states of psychotic depression and despair; female monkeys are impregnated on a "rape rack" at the Wisconsin Regional Primate Center in Madison, after which they turn on their offspring with a vengeance. The researcher who conducted this experiment said that one of the mothers' "favorite tricks was to crush the infant's skull with their teeth." "A really sickening behavior pattern," he added, "was that of smashing the infant's face to the floor and rubbing it back and forth." But at the end of a related study, he said: "Buoyed by these results, we have continued to search for techniques to produce depression in monkeys. [It is] essential to realize that the findings of such work hold implication for human depression only at the level of analogy."

Many other animals are sacrificed in a process more immediately relevant to man—the large-scale testing of cosmetics and drugs. Before each new drug is approved for prescription, it must be tested for side effects on generation after generation of laboratory animals. When a toxic chemical, such as a pesticide, is being screened for licensing, its "Lethal Dose 50" must be established—the level at which it will kill half the experimental animals, leaving the rest very sick indeed. When a new cosmetic is prepared for the market, it must first be painted onto the eyes of laboratory rabbits, their legs pinioned and their eyelids clipped open, to see what effect it has there.

There is a factional division within the animal liberation forces on this point. Some, like Peter Singer, say that the answer is to stop developing new products that require animal tests. We should eschew such frivolities as new cosmetics, he says, and, "make do without new nonessential drugs." Not surprisingly, this proposal has brought a response from the scientific community. Last spring, Steven Weisbroth, the head of the Laboratory Animal Resources Division of the State University of New York at Stony Brook, wrote in the New York *Times* that

. . . the majority of animals used in a research context in this country are used . . . to gain information about the effects on humans of materials, procedures, agents, and chemicals by first exposing them to animals. It is a form of consumer protection that as a society we are determined to support.

We have two choices, according to Singer: return to the Stone Age and do without these products, or accept the thalidomides and other toxic consequences of inadequately investigated products. I believe any sane person would prefer to accept the necessity for animal investigations to protect human health.

(The animal forces are always delighted to hear about thalidomide, because it is a point for their side. Far from revealing the risk of birth defects, thalidomide tests on animals showed it to be safe; the hazards appeared only after humans started using the drug. "Not only is the laboratory torture cruel," says Eleanor Seiling, "but often the results can't be extrapolated to humans.")

Other factions in the animals' rights movement, led by the UAA, have emphasized a different solution to the laboratory problem—not abandoning the experiments, but using a different sort of experimental subject. The UAA has collected an enormous literature on alternate methods of experimentation, making another prima facie case that the toll of rats and dogs might easily be reduced.

Over the last ten years, the scientific journals have reported increasingly frequent tests upon "tissue cultures"— cells from the human (or animal) liver, brain, skin, or other organs which have been removed during biopsies or surgery and kept alive *in vitro.* Experimenters have managed to addict these cultures to narcotics, instead of addicting live monkeys. They have used the cultures to test the side effects of drugs, the damage done by radiation, and the mechanics of metabolism. Frozen eyes from eye banks have been used for tests of irritating chemicals, like those now performed on live rabbits. Many other methods, according to United Action for Animals, need only a little attention before they, too, will be ready for us. As one of the UAA pamphlets says, in rather typical prose

NON-ANIMAL USING RESEARCH METHODS [are] waiting to be used as soon as our government can be persuaded to direct research funds into THESE HUMANE ALTERNATIVES instead of the CONTINUED TORTURE OF LIVE ANIMALS.

If these "humane alternatives" do work, then time, money, and legislation may reduce the wear and tear on laboratory animals. (UAA wants stipulations in federal research grants that the alternate methods will be used wherever possible.) But even then human judgment will have its place. If Benting and Best had felt, early in the century, that the only way to develop insulin was to deprive dogs of their pancreases, we would not have wanted a United Action for Animals breathing down their necks. Of the many specialized crannies where research continues today, it is hard for outsiders to say which will prove similarly beneficial fifty years from now.

So the animals' fate will rest, to a large extent, with tomorrow's scientists; certainly today's hardly blink before using frogs and mice. Several medical school administrators told me that more and more of their students are grumbling about dissections. Why, they ask, should one hundred students observe the circulation in one hundred dogs, when a film of one dog would educate them all? And students who, when in high school, spare the lives of amoebae may, twenty years from now, take more pains with their guinea pigs. A new day may be coming for the beasts of field, farm, and lab—if this year's radical issue does not fade as quickly as its predecessors.

ANIMAL RIGHTS: NIH CAT SEX STUDY[3]

A public relations disaster has settled like a poisonous fog over the American Museum of Natural History in New York and seems to grow thicker with every attempt to dispel it.

The cause of the disaster is a study of cats performed by two of the museum's investigators. For 15 years they have been analyzing the animals' sexual behavior by the standard physiological procedures of removing glands, nerves, or brain tissue. But news of the study came only recently to the attention of New York's many animal lovers, since when the museum has been sandbagged with just about every item in the public relations consultant's book of horrors. Almost every weekend for the last 3 months there have been picket lines or demonstrations held outside the museum's stately quarters overlooking Central Park. Newspaper coverage of the affair has ranged from the critical to the unreservedly hostile, delivered under headlines such as "Cats Are Tortured in Vicious Experiments at Famous N.Y.C. Museum" (*National Enquirer*), "Museum Ends Its Silence on Study of Cat Sex Lives" (New York *Times*), and "Congress Pays for Sex Sadism at Museum" (*Our Town*).

With help of this kind, the affair has swollen to national

[3] Article entitled "Animal Rights: NIH Cat Sex Study Brings Grief to New York Museum," by Nicholas Wade, member of the News and Comment staff. *Science.* 194:162–7. O. 8, '76. Copyright © 1976 by the American Association for the Advancement of Science. All rights reserved. Reprinted with permission.

proportions. Protests at the experiment have arrived from all over the country in a growing torrent—400 letters in June, 650 in July, and about 1500 in August. Some 30 congressmen have inquired about the study in response to constituents' complaints. Representative Hamilton Fish of New York wrote to the museum to say he was "personally appalled to learn that such experiments have been going on for 15 years," and another [former] New York Representative, Edward Koch, came up with an interesting example of the non-smear smear technique. "While I am not prepared at this moment to label the kind of experimentation as Nazi-like, it does recall the barbarities of the Nazis," he wrote in a letter to the Secretary of Health, Education, and Welfare.

The affair has brought the museum bomb threats and threats to kill or maim the staff involved in the study. Though these have not materialized, a more tangible threat is the vigorous campaign by the animal rights groups to reach the museum's sources of the support. Picket lines have been thrown up to persuade the public not to enter, and letters written to the museum's members, donors, and trustees. Little support has been lost so far—some 60 people have canceled their membership and one benefactress has cut the museum out of her will—but the long-term effect on the museum's image may prove more serious. "Clearly our reputation is being damaged," says the museum director Thomas D. Nicholson.

The museum's plight carries a warning for other institutions whose experiments with animals are susceptible to being made the focus of public passions. The animal rights groups are particularly well informed about the cat study because, through the Freedom of Information Act, they obtained all the investigator's grant applications from the National Institutes of Health. Second, the issue of animal rights has been taken up recently by several young philosophers whose writings have injected a new intellectual vigor into the movement. The animal rights groups believe that there is a historical trend in their favor which goes from minorities' rights, to women's rights, to animal rights. The attack on the American Museum of Natural History is just the first shot in what they hope will be a broader campaign.

The museum, however, was picked on first because it is a particularly vulnerable target. Most people are surprised to learn that any experiments at all are carried on there. That the study is on a species of household pet, and concerns sexual behavior, both topics which most people have little difficulty in relating to, has also made the study harder to explain and defend to the public.

The chief architect of the museum's discomfiture is Henry Spira, a New York high school teacher and free-lance journalist. Spira noticed an abstract of the cat study in a list of animal experiments disapproved of by United Action for Animals. His action in obtaining the grant applications under the Freedom of Information Act was crucial because it brought to light a wealth of detail about the study that would not otherwise have been available.

The chief investigator for the project is Lester R. Aronson, the curator of the museum's department of animal behavior and one of the early pioneers in developing the quantitative study of sexual behavior. With his assistant, Madeline L. Cooper, he has been probing the sexual behavior of domestic cats for almost two decades, mostly with the support of the National Institute of Child Health and Human Development (NICHD). NIH funding of the project has totaled $412,143 over the last 15 years.

The general method of the study has been to observe the behavioral changes that ensue from depriving the cats of various kinds of sensation or brain function. The grant applications describe experiments that call for such operations as destruction of the cochlea, section of the optic nerve, ablation of the olfactory bulb, lesioning of the amygdala, deafferentation of the penis, and castration.

In plainer language, of course, this means that the experimenters planned to deafen the cats, blind them, destroy their sense of smell, remove parts of the brain, sever the nerves in the penis, and cut off their testicles. (The experiments requiring the cats to be blinded and deafened were in fact never carried out.) To those not inured to the practices of experimental psychology, it sounds like no picnic.

Spira is not an all-the-way antivivisectionist, like many in the animal rights movement, but he believes that for the purposes of many experiments the scientist can use alternatives to live animals, and that the killing of live animals in school room demonstrations is brutalizing and unnecessary. When he received Aronson's grant applications from the NIH in August last year, he saw the cat study as an ideal vehicle for advancing the cause. He showed the documents to the New York *Times*, which was not interested in the story at that stage, and then to various animal rights groups.

"There's a room you will never enter at the American Museum of Natural History. It's filled with suffering animals—and your tax money is paying for it. Demand an end to the experimentation and animal suffering."

So began a widely circulated leaflet put out by the Society for Animal Rights. Friends of Animals took out a full page ad in the New York *Post* to say:

Believe it or not, they're torturing cats and kittens at the American Museum of Natural History. . . .
Why? For what purpose?
For crude, absurd sex experiments. Paid for with our tax dollars. So that researchers can study the sexual performance of crippled cats.
And toward what goal?
There is none. It is simply "experimentation" for its own sake.

Spira himself wrote a series of articles on the subject for *Our Town*, a weekly Manhattan newspaper, arguing that Aronson's experiments were "crude and routine" and unlikely to produce any new knowledge. "It's not a question of giant medical breakthroughs; nor balancing whether animals should suffer or people; but a way of getting government grants in exchange for animals' agony and blood. Congress should be forced to choose between the greed of the vivisectors and the real needs of our society," Spira stated.

The animal rights groups were thus able to get their side of the case well publicized in the media. In fact, to a surprising extent, they are the media. The president of Friends of Animals is Cleveland Amory, a columnist and broadcaster. Head of the Vivisection Investigation League is Pegeen Fitzgerald, who has a daily radio show on WOR radio. "There is not a day when we are not talking about animal matters," she says. Fitzgerald, Spira, and Ed Kayatt, editor of *Our Town*, have formed a steering committee whose aim is to have the museum close down not only Aronson's experiment but the whole department of animal behavior.

Given the nature of the experiment, and its critics' entrenchment in the media, the museum had clearly been dealt a poor hand. But in retrospect at least, it seems to have played diffidently even the cards it had. At first authorities refused to let Aronson speak to the press or allow reporters to visit his laboratory. When the museum finally yielded and reporters found only a roomful of frolicsome felines instead of the soundproof torture chamber they had been led to expect, their suspicion was so rampant that even the New York *Times* implied the place had been cleaned up the night before.

Asked by the NIH for a review of its animal welfare procedures, the museum authorities, instead of getting an independent committee to write them a clean bill of health, turned to a group which consisted only of people with ties to the museum, and which included Aronson, Cooper, and the consulting veterinarian to the project.

The museum's few public statements have been couched in general terms, in contrast to the detail-laden accusations of the animal rights groups, and it has also shifted its main defense of the project from arguing that all basic research is important to contending that the cat study "relates closely to human problems."

The animal rights groups' case rests chiefly on three contentions, that the cats are inhumanely treated quite apart from the needs of the experiment, that the experimental manipulations are cruel and ethically unacceptable, and that the experiment itself is unlikely to lead to any significant new knowledge.

The belief that the cats have been kept inhumanely stems from statements in Aronson's grant applications, such as the reference to a "transfer cage" for handling violent animals. Aronson explains he asked for the cage because he planned to make a certain brain lesion which is said in the literature to make animals aggressive. (In fact, like the proposals to blind and deafen cats, the experiment was never performed.)

As for the famous soundproof room, the museum in a public statement denies that it exists. It does exist—the grant applications describe a "sound retarded" testing room—but its purpose is to insulate the experiment from outside noises rather than to muffle the screams of tortured cats.

Aronson's cats have every appearance of being well treated, it is in the interests of the experiment to keep them as well as possible, and the numerous outside inspections of the laboratory have never found any evidence of the cats being poorly housed, fed, or cared for. This charge may confidently be said to be groundless.

Whether the experiments themselves can be said to be cruel is a judgment that may be influenced by the perceived worth of the experiment, the greater its value the more justifiable being the harm done to the cat. While none of the manipulations (proposed or actually done) would have done the cats any good, operations such as castration are not unique to Aronson's lab but are the fate of many a household pet. The allegations by the animal rights groups that the experimenters took a sadistic pleasure in the experiments is an obvious absurdity. Aronson says that surgery was conducted under anesthesia, as is customary, and the animal rights groups have offered no evidence for doubting the statement. On the other hand, the public outcry about the experiments stems from the difference between what the experimental psychologist and the ordinary person would instinctively regard as cruel.

The third charge, that the experiments are useless, raises an issue of some complexity. The project seems to have started out as purely basic research. Only in the most recent application, that of 1974, is there reference to specific clinical problems, the control of oversexuality and undersexuality. Since the clinical relevance of the study has come to be asserted only recently, perhaps reflecting the changing public atttiudes toward the funding of science, it is probably as basic research that the cat study should be judged.

As evidence of its merit the museum and the NICHD

point to the fact that it has been reviewed and recommended for support four times by the NIH's peer review system. Peer review committees are composed of the nation's leading experts in the field and it is difficult to second-guess their judgment. But one kind of second opinion is offered by the Science Citation Index, which annually lists for each article the times it has been cited in the scientific literature that year. Of the 21 articles that Aronson and his colleagues have published on the cat study since 1962, 14 have never been cited in the scientific literature between 1965, when the Science Citation Index starts, and March 1976. Because of the short citation half-life of scientific papers, it is unlikely that they ever will be cited. The seven other papers have an average 5.6 citations each over the same 11-year period.

If a paper is never cited—as indeed is the fate of about half the scientific articles published—it is hard to make the case that it has contributed in any important respect to the advance of knowledge. On the other hand it is easy to argue the importance, for example, of a classic paper on monkeys which Aronson published in 1934 but which is still regularly cited. (Most of Aronson's work has been on fish, the cat study taking only a third of his time.)

Yet the project may have received fewer citations than others of comparable merit simply because few people conduct this kind of work on cats. "Aronson is in a single investigator field," says William A. Sadler, the NICHD project officer and an articulate defender of the study. According to Aronson, "Most of the research on reproduction is in rats and the rat people are very parochial in that they only read the rat literature and only cite rat studies, so very frequently our papers are not cited."

Whatever the citation rate of the cat study, the animal rights groups' campaign has been a harsh ordeal for Aronson and Cooper. Aronson, who is aged 66 and has been planning in any case to retire soon, is an established and productive scientist whose work, in the aspects for which it is being assailed, differs in no way from the research carried on by a great many other investigators.

Even the animal rights groups concede this point in their

own way. "Aronson is no different from thousands of others," says Eleanor Seiling, the indefatigable force behind United Action for Animals. Seiling, in whose bulletin the Aronson study was first brought to the animal groups' attention, believes that the "vendetta" against Aronson is futile. "I want something done not just about the museum, I want to change the system," she says.

Whether the animal rights groups have the power to change the system is open to doubt. Most of them are essentially one-person organizations, each bitterly jealous of the others. Even the crowd-drawing campaign against the museum has been marked by a feud between the Society for Animal Rights and a loose coalition of 11 other groups. The Society for Animal Rights held its meetings on different dates and has now ceased to demonstrate altogether because more aggressively minded groups prevented its demonstrations from being orderly. About the only unifying factor among the various groups is their dislike for [now former] Representative Koch, who has introduced legislation in Congress to set up a commission on the humane treatment of animals. The animal groups accuse him of using the museum affair to gain publicity for himself. They make similar accusations of each other. For example the Society for Animal Rights, whose expenses last year exceeded its revenues by $136,000, has been criticized for attacking the museum and soliciting donations in the same advertisement.

Another impediment to political influence, besides their lack of unity, is the extreme nature of the positions taken by the various groups. Between the out-and-out antivivisection position of the Vivisection Investigation League and the viewpoint of United Action for Animals that virtually all experimental animals can be replaced by nonliving alternatives, there is little chance for a more moderate and generally persuasive doctrine to emerge.

On the other hand, the animal rights groups believe that the tide of the times is moving in their favor. They believe that the same sense of justice and humanity which animated the sentiment for minorities' rights and then for women's rights will eventually be asserted on behalf of animals, both those used in laboratories and those killed for meat. "People are widening the sphere of their consciousness," says Nancy Stassinopoulos of the Society for Animal Rights; "They are better informed and better educated, and they are perceiving man's place in nature and his relationship toward animals in a different light."

The issue of animal rights has recently been taken up by people from outside the mainstream animal lovers, such as philosophers. For example Robert Nozick of Harvard, whose *Anarchy, State and Utopia* has received rave reviews from his colleagues, devotes a section of the book to animal rights. While Nozick does not specifically address the use of animals in experiments, he considers that animals should count for something, and for enough at least that they should not even be eaten. "The extra benefits Americans today gain from eating animals do not justify doing it," Nozick concludes. . . .

Researchers use a surprisingly large number of animals—some 63 million a year in the United States alone, according to one estimate, a figure which includes 85,000 primates, 500,000 dogs, 200,000 cats, and 45 million rodents. When the right nerve is touched, the issue can arouse strong public passions, as the Aronson study has shown. A similar case in 1973, involving the Department of Defense's use of beagles, brought the House Armed Services Committee more mail than it had received on any event since Truman sacked General McArthur. Does the public appeal of the animal rights issue depend only on misplaced sentiment, or is there an argument somewhere there to be answered?

Sadism Frowned On

While most researchers doubtless respect the interests of their animals as much as possible, the codes of practice governing animal experimentation do not concede that animals have any rights whatever that should weigh against the purposes of the experimenter. The statements of principles issued by the American Psychological Association (APA) and the

National Society for Medical Research simply require that animals be well kept (which is generally in the researcher's own interest). The principles implicitly embody an absolute freedom by the researcher to use animals however he will. In fact the greatest moral burden laid on the experimenter by the APA is not to be positively sadistic: "Research procedures subjecting animals to discomfort shall be conducted only when such discomfort is required, and is justified by the objectives of the research," says the code which the APA's council of representatives found worth approving.

Just as the researcher is not required or formally encouraged to make animals count for anything in the design of his experiment, so the peer review system makes no formal attempt to balance the worth of an experiment against the interests of the animals whose lives it would take. Study sections are instructed to consider proposals on their scientific merit alone. Thus an experiment of minor merit requiring a hecatomb of animals might in theory receive a favorable mark. In practice, study sections do turn down experiments that surpass a certain combination of harshness and triviality. Keith Murray, executive secretary of the NIH's experimental psychology study section, says that there have been occasional instances when an application was turned down because of unnecessary cruelty. He cites as an example a proposal, which the investigator submitted three or four times, to blind infant monkeys in order to study how well their mothers looked after them.

A practical test of one's treatment of others is reciprocity. What if the Andromedans arrived (a question posed in essence by Nozick), demonstrated that they were as intellectually superior to us as we are to animals, and said that they regretted that they would have to use a few million humans in a basic research project of quite considerable merit? The APA's code of principles would not be much of a fence to hide behind.

"Surely one day," Singer observes in *Animal Liberation*, "our children's children, reading about what was done in laboratories in the 20th century, will feel the same sense of horror and incredulity at what otherwise civilized people can do that we now feel when we read about the atrocities of the Roman gladiatorial arenas or the 18th-century slave trade." The projection may sound far fetched, yet history teaches that only fashion in clothes changes faster than fashions in ethics.

ANIMAL WELFARE AND SCIENTIFIC RESEARCH[4]

Nicholas Wade's article "Animal rights: NIH cat sex study brings grief to New York museum" [p 87] requires a response because of its profound significance for science, and also because it is necessary to correct several substantive statements. Wade states, for example, that when the National Institutes of Health (NIH) asked the American Museum of Natural History for a special review of its animal welfare procedures, "instead of getting an independent committee to write them a clean bill of health," the Museum "turned to a group which consisted only of people with ties to the Museum. . . ." Wade fails to say that, in constituting this committee, the Museum followed *exactly* the instructions of NIH. This procedure, which the Museum has followed regularly and for many years, was clearly approved in a special report prepared by the NIH Animal Welfare Officer, Roy Kinard. Further, in response to a request by the Museum administration, William A. Sadler, chief of the Population and Reproduction Grants Branch of the National Institute of Child Health and Human Development, appointed an ad hoc committee consisting of Sadler and two leading research veterinarians, one from Harvard University and the other from the Oak Ridge National Laboratory. A detailed report of this committee was inserted by New York Congressman Edward

[4] Letter to the Editor submitted by Lester R. Aronson and Madeline L. Cooper, Department of Animal Behavior, American Museum of Natural History, New York. *Science.* 194:784. N. 19, '76. Copyright © 1976 by the American Association for the Advancement of Science. Reprinted with permission.

Koch into the *Congressional Record* of 24 August 1976 which
gave unqualified approval to all of our research procedures.

Wade describes one of the leaders of the actions against
our institution, Henry Spira, as ". . . not an all-the-way antivivisectionist." In Spira's writings, repeated references are
made to "mutilations" and "butchering" by the "greedy vivisectors" of "millions" of "defenseless animals." Spira men-
tions specifically rats, mice, hamsters, rabbits, guinea pigs,
birds, monkeys, and innocent beings, that are "being driven
insane, suffocated, poisoned, battered, radiated, crushed,
blinded, scalded." In none of his articles does Spira acknowledge that any animal should ever be used for any experiment,
no matter how crucial it may be judged to be for human welfare or survival. How much further is "all-the-way"?

Moreover, Wade devotes roughly one-third of the article
to some of the rationale of the antivivisectionist movement
such as the simplistic, reductionist idea that "alternatives to
live animals," for example, research with computers, test
tubes, and tissue cultures, can be substituted for animal experiments, and to the quasi-moralistic claim that animals
have "rights" equal to the sociopolitical rights of women and
minorities. Wade does not indicate that many see such statements as being antiscience and, in fact, fails to present any of
the opposing views.

In Wade's effort to judge the value of our research on sex
behavior of cats, he brushes aside the repeatedly favorable
decisions of several peer review committees ("it is difficult to
second-guess their judgment") and chooses as his sole criterion of scientific worthiness the number of citations in *Science
Citation Index.* Of the 21 publications to which Wade refers,
the seven full reports, each representing 3 to 5 years of continuous experimental observation, have all been cited except
for one which was published in Moscow. In addition, two
doctoral dissertations by former students have been cited as
such, and later as journal publications. The remaining 14
publications were abstracts of reports given at scientific
meetings while the work was in progress, and even a goodly
number of these have been cited. As Eugene Garfield, father

of the *Science Citation Index,* has emphasized, the index can only serve as a valid criterion if its limitations are recognized and it is used properly.

We believe that the criteria for the morality and ethics of research must include its significance for human welfare, but the statements made by critics of the moral and ethical aspects of our work raise doubts about their values in this respect. How much suffering does one allow, how many human lives and how many pets does one sacrifice in the name of the "rights" of discarded and unwanted cats and dogs or laboratory-raised animals? On the order of one million unwanted cats and dogs are destroyed each year in animal pounds, their use denied to legitimate research institutions. Wade chooses not to discuss these fundamental aspects of the problem. Ironically, we find ourselves in agreement with the antivivisectionists on one point. They are distributing copies of Wade's article, which they view as supporting their cause.

The AAAS, as the most representative organization of scientists in the country, is obligated to respond to the anti-science, anti-intellectual, and inhuman position taken by our critics.

ANIMALS AND ETHICS[5]

The letters from Aronson and Cooper and from Sachs [p 101] take exception to several statements in Wade's article on the cat experiments at the American Museum of Natural History. The letters are, unfortunately, in no way unusual in their failure to face squarely the broader ethical issues involved in animal experimentation. Speaking of Henry Spira, one of the leaders of the action against the museum, Aronson and Cooper remark: "In none of his articles does Spira acknowledge that any animal should ever be used for any ex-

[5] Letter to the Editor, submitted by Marjorie Anchel, New York Botanical Garden, Bronx, NY. *Science.* 195:131. Ja. 14, '77. Copyright © 1977, by the American Association for the Advancement of Science. Reprinted with permission.

periment, no matter how crucial it may be judged for human welfare or survival." If it is true that Spira has deliberately evaded the problem, this is a valid criticism. By the same token, it is incumbent on scientists not to deserve the converse criticism: "In none of their writings do they acknowledge that any experiment should not be done, regardless of how much suffering it entails for the animals used."

Aronson and Cooper refer to the "simplistic, reductionist idea that 'alternatives to live animals' . . . can be substituted for animal experiments. . . ." and to the "quasi-moralistic claim that animals have 'rights' equal to the sociopolitical rights of women and minorities." They complain that Wade does not indicate that "many see such statements as being antiscience." I would like to point out that most of the "alternatives to live animals" (many of which are used very successfully in some areas) were developed for purely pragmatic, not humane, reasons; that evaluating the "rights" of living things, far from being an obvious and simple decision, is a difficult philosophical problem; and that raising moral questions is not "antiscience."

Sachs states that "The public's right to challenge the ethics and economics of animal research is unquestioned." He then goes on to say: "The present peer review system, as fallible as it may be, has been largely successful in curbing unethical excesses and in fitting research priorities to available funds." The peer review system, to my knowledge, is devoted almost exclusively to determining the scientific merit of a proposal and the capability of an investigator to carry it out. The "economics" (funding) of the proposal is considered also. But the review committees, regrettably, do not include members designated specifically as spokesmen for the experimental animals, to "challenge the ethics . . ." of the proposed research.

ANIMAL RESEARCH DEFENSE[6]

The demonstrations against the animal behavior research at the American Museum of Natural History are potentially damaging at several levels. First, there is the potential damage to the public reputations of Lester Aronson and Madeline Cooper. Those who are unfamiliar with their research may wonder whether it justified the cost in dollars and animal lives. However, Aronson and Cooper will continue to be regarded highly by their scientific colleagues. Few scientists have contributed more to making us aware of the complex interactions between behavioral experience and the neurological and hormonal control of behavior.

Their recent work on the amygdala demonstrates that some widely held opinions on the function of this important part of the brain are wrong, partly because these opinions derived from research less sophisticated than that characteristic of Aronson and Cooper. Next, there is the potential damage to the Museum's Department of Animal Behavior. Since the late 1930s, this department has had a major influence on the conceptualization of human and animal behavior. Several of this nation's leading behavioral scientists were trained there and the department's academic progeny are now teaching and doing laboratory and field research around the world. Under the curatorships of Frank A. Beach, T. C. Schneirla, and Lester Aronson, the department became a center of the "epigenetic" view of development, a theory which emphasizes that each stage of an organism's development results from a dynamic interaction between the organism and its environment. This view served as antithesis to the more preferred mationistic thesis of classical European ethology. If there is a current synthesis it emerged from the interaction between the epigeneticists and the classical ethologists.

[6] Letter to the Editor, submitted by Dr. Benjamin D. Sachs, Department of Psychology, University of Connecticut (Storrs). *Science.* 194:786. N. 19, '76. Copyright © 1976, by the American Association for the Advancement of Science. Reprinted with permission. Title supplied by the Editor.

The broadest potential impact of the antivivisectionists is to reduce or eliminate the use of animals, or at least domestic animals and primates, in basic and applied biomedical research. Since these animals are often the most appropriate physiological models, the outcome would be to terminate research that cannot be initiated with humans. To the extent that this broad goal is achieved human health and human knowledge may pay a terrible price.

The public's right to challenge the ethics and economics of animal research is unquestioned. The present peer review system, as fallible as it may be, has been largely successful in curbing unethical excesses and in fitting research priority to available funds. Until a better system is developed, the peer review process should prevail.

One final note. Ten years ago, *Science* rejected, without review, a report by Aronson and Cooper because the editor felt that the sex research on cats, as described in that report, would offend the sensibilities of some *Science* readers including antivivisectionists. Ultimately *Science* had the report reviewed and published a modified version (8 Ap. '66, p 226) with no adverse repercussions. To spite the superficial sexual enlightenment of the last decade, the current reaction to the sexual aspects of the research of Aronson and Cooper and many of their colleagues indicates that, for many persons, basic research on sexual behavior is still beyond the pale. As Wade suggests sex research tends to gain notoriety easily, no matter how ethically it may be conceived and executed.

ANIMAL RIGHTS ADVOCATE URGES NEW DEAL[7]

The animal rights movement, which for long had as its major champions the proverbial "little old ladies in tennis shoes," has in recent years achieved a new level of intellectual sophistication and political effectiveness.

[7] Article by Constance Holden, contributing editor. *Science.* 201:35. Jl. 7, '78.
Copyright © 1978, by the American Association for the Advancement of Science. All rights reserved. Reprinted with permission.

The movement has its own philosophers and theorists. One is an English-born veterinarian, psychologist, and author named Michael Fox, who for the past 18 months has been director of the Humane Society's new Institute for the Study of Animal Problems in Washington, D.C.

The institute is the research arm of the society. "My being here is a symptom of a new direction in the humane movement," says Fox. "Sentiment is not enough" as an argument for humane treatment of animals. "We can't use the argument that animal suffering is reason to be humane," for that after all is our own subjective judgment. It also implies that there is a cutoff point somewhere—that baby seals, for example, deserve more respect than lizards. That is a form of "speciesism" which Fox deplores. "We have to be ethically responsible because they exist—not because they are sentient."

The institute, which has four research associates, is engaged in gathering good hard Western-minded scientific evidence to undergird the ethic it embraces, which is more in tune with the spiritual doctrines of the East.

A major concern is the use of animals in laboratories and schools. Although the Animal Welfare Act of 1970 promulgates standards for the care of lab animals, it says nothing about their behavioral and social well-being. Yet, Fox says, humane treatment is better science because you cannot get good results with emotionally deprived animals. For example, he says, the LD_{50} (dose at which half a population dies) for rats kept in separate cages is different from that for animals kept in their own social group. Although Fox is mainly concerned with primates, dogs, cats, and rodents, he says that even with fish there are data showing that social deprivation limits growth of nerve cell dendrites.

Fox's group also contends that a great deal of unnecessary research is being done on animals—testing cosmetics on rabbits' eyes, for example, or shaving cats' faces to test skin lotion. In many of these instances the animal testing is irrelevant to humans, and there are alternatives—testing substances on tissue cultures or using human volunteers—that are both more reliable and more humane. "The research establishment is beginning to face up to the issue quite squarely," says Fox, "provided we don't scream abolitionist or antivivisectionist nonsense." The institute will be doing more work on alternatives to animal subjects when its newest staff member, Andrew Rowan, arrives from England. Rowan, an Oxford graduate and former Rhodes scholar, has been working in London for the Fund for the Replacement of Animals in Medical Experiments.

Another area where people are behaving very badly, says Fox, involves high school science fairs. Children are doing stupid and ill-supervised experiments, such as dosing rats with lead or scalding them, or putting saltwater fish in fresh water. One child's project consisted of evaluating the effects of his mother's Valium and Thorazine on a hamster. "They are still giving dogs strychnine at some schools to see how it works," adds Fox. Science fairs have been a long-standing source of outrage among the animal rights types, but according to Fox only one state—California—effectively regulates these practices.

But the most large-scale outrage—and Fox is glad he is almost through with this project because it takes its toll emotionally—has to do with the treatment of animals raised for food. Animals are beginning to get some legal rights, namely through the Animal Welfare Act and the Endangered Species Act, but farm animals "are a totally neglected area."

Fox has traveled the country inspecting animals on "factory farms" and is now completing a book, tentatively entitled *Animal Farm Revisited.* His basic case is that massive animal rearing operations are not only inhumane, but by no means as efficient as their advanced technology and economies of scale might indicate. Half the country's antibiotics are fed to farm animals, he says, and much of this is unnecessary as they are administered to counter diseases that would not occur if the animals were not subjected to overcrowding and stress. Special diets and genetic selection to enhance meat quality or augment production also serve to weaken animals' natural coping mechanisms. Calves raised for veal, for example, suffer anemia and weakness from their low-iron diet: also, because they are fed no roughage, they resort to licking off their own hair.

Behavioral problems are legion as a result of overcrowding and lack of normal opportunities for socialization. Pigs chew each other's tails off. Chicks have their beaks cut off so they will not peck each other. Pigs and chickens even resort to cannibalism. Animals kept tethered in solitary pens become unbalanced from boredom, chew on themselves, molt excessively, and develop nervous tics and stereotyped behaviors; hogs and bulls, which are used for artifical insemination, often become sterile because of lack of social contact; this is treated by more hormones.

Fox says the mortality rate is as high as 20 percent on some farms, and many more deaths occur in the course of transporting animals for fattening and slaughtering. He says that the ventilation and temperature control on the trucks are haphazard, and losses in transportation alone amount to $1 billion a year—equivalent to a 4-mile-long freight train filled with carcasses.

Fox says many of the inhumanities could be altered by simple means—supplying places for nesting and roosting for hens, for example, or changing the concrete flooring that causes pigs to develop arthritis, or supplying shaded areas in beef feedlots.

Fox talks much of the need for "empathy" with animals. By this he does not mean anthropomorphism, but rather a replacement of "macho dominionism"—with its assumption that humans have a right to control and dominate the rest of nature—with the recognition that all life is valuable.

III.   ANIMALS IN EDUCATION AND SCIENCE

EDITOR'S INTRODUCTION

In the realm of animal behavior, there is evidence not only that many animals are capable of complex language systems and behavior patterns, but also that this behavior, when properly understood, can be of enormous benefit to humans. The notion that animals are inferior to humans was set back with the discovery that dolphins, whales and some primates can actually communicate "human" concepts in their own ways.

The first three articles in this section deal with observing, documenting, and using the senses in which animals excel. Melba and David Caldwell, research scientists writing in *Sea Frontiers* about their work with Bottlenosed dolphins, describe the ability of these animals to "communicate," through clicks, barks, whistles, and other noises that express human emotions such as threat, protest, and irritation.

The animal behavior that Phylis Magida discusses in the second article, reprinted from *International Wildlife*, is a phenomenon of great scientific potential for humans, if we can learn to detect the sensory and extra-sensory mechanism that certain animals possess for predicting drastic changes in the environment, or impending disaster, such as earthquakes or storms. Writing in the Washington *Post*, George C. Wilson, author of the third selection, describes a U.S. Navy program in which trained pigeons, with their superior eyesight, consistently outperformed human spotters in sighting people lost at sea.

The next three selections deal with the manipulation of animal behavior in order to learn more about human behavior. Daniel Jack Chasan, writing in *Smithsonian*, relates some of the scientific advantages of behavior modification at the Portland Zoo. The operant conditioning of diana monkeys clearly demonstrates the interrelatedness of all living things. In the fifth article, reprinted from the Washington *Post*, this theory is further advanced by Lois Timnick, who worked in the West Indies with groups of brain-damaged monkeys, "close relatives of man," in order to learn about ourselves from such research.

The final article, by Beth Nissen writing in the *Wall Street Journal*, tells how Animal Behavior Enterprises modifies animal behavior for entertainment. Animals are trained to perform impossible, often absurd tasks.

COMMUNICATION IN ATLANTIC BOTTLENOSED DOLPHINS[1]

Recent discoveries in the field of animal communication have shown that many species possess highly sophisticated systems for transmitting messages to their own kind. The most startling revelations have appeared from studies of social animals. Bees, termites, and wolves, as well as humans, are examples of such animals.

The Atlantic bottlenosed dolphin (*Tursiops truncatus*) also has a tightly knit, cooperative social structure, and so a similarly complex system of information exchange in this species would be expected. These expectations appear to be justified, particularly in the area of sound communication.

Unfortunately, it seems impossible for people to hear the word "communication" without surrounding it with all of the implications that the word has for our own species. This is a natural reaction, but it does degrade the term to the narrow spectrum of sound and even further to an intensely small area called "speech." Insofar as it is known, this particular bizarre capability has evolved in only one species—man.

[1] Article by Melba C. and David K. Caldwell, research scientists at the Biocommunication and Marine Mammal Research Facility, University of Florida. *Sea Frontiers*. 25:130–9. My. '79. Copyright © 1979 by International Oceanographic Foundation. All rights reserved. Reprinted with permission.

Whatever the reason, all other animals exchange information nonverbally. Although their communications are limited largely to the "here and now," this is obviously all that is needed for them to get along beautifully—in many ways better than the poor benighted human who is daily inundated with lies, half-truths, rationalizations, and government paperwork.

A *Variety of Sound Signals*

Dolphins do depend heavily on the use of sound in transmitting information. Unlike ambient light, which is operative only a portion of the day and virtually useless underwater, sound energy is a usable channel 24 hours a day even underwater. Sound additionally carries for long distances underwater where the speed of transmission is four times faster than in air. Dolphins have evolved several types of sound which they use with considerable finesse.

It has been postulated, and probably correctly, that when the ancestors of dolphins reentered the water that they brought with them the basic mammalian sound repertoire. These are of the pulsed type and include barks, squeaks, and squawks. Insofar as we know, these carry about the same messages as they do in terrestrial mammals. These are sounds of threat, protest, and irritation. As the level of emotion rises, the number and loudness of the sounds also rise. In addition, they shift in more subtle ways. The dominant frequency and/or number of pulses per second increases or decreases with emotional excitation or inhibition. Signals of this type that are not discrete but gradually change from one to the other are called "graded signals." Although words are discrete signals, humans make considerable use of graded signals. A mother calling her child in for dinner uses a considerably less intense vocalization than she does if the child is engaged in a dangerous pursuit. Children learn to recognize these gradations very quickly, and probably before they learn words.

When dolphins are in an extreme state of alarm or conflict, they emit a sharp forceful "crack" sound. This "alarm crack" is ideally suited for carrying long distances underwater and alerting the other members of the group that there is danger in the area. These certainly represent an "attention getter" of the highest order. We have been listening to dolphins with our earphones and hydrophone when the animals cut loose with a few of these intensely forceful sounds and have been as startled as by a loud thunder clap.

Clicks and Echoes

Dolphins have elevated pulsed sounds into a system of exquisitely refined clicks over which they have control. The animals adjust the intensity, number per second, and dominant frequencies with great precision to obtain from the echoes the information that they need about the environment. Loud, low-frequency clicks are emitted when the animal is orienting itself or making a simple discrimination. If the object being "viewed" by a dolphin is small and in need of close inspection, the animal emits rapid-fire, high-frequency clicks. One dolphin, which spontaneously amused itself by playing with these sounds, could shift back and forth between the various types of clicks in fractions of a second. The shifts that it made were done so rapidly that some of them appeared to have been emitted virtually simultaneously.

A Whistle of Its Own

Dolphins make another type of sound that is quite different from what is normally heard in terrestrial mammals. This is a pleasant whistle which sounds similar to some bird calls. Dolphins apparently use these whistles to keep in touch with the other members of their group. Each member of a dolphin school has a whistle of its own—called its "signature whistle." Dolphins learn to recognize each other's whistles so well that with a little practice they can correctly identify another animal's whistle with only ½ second of listening time. Once an individual has developed its own particularly distinctive signature whistle, a process that takes a year or two depending on the individual infant dolphin, it appears to keep it certainly for many years and probably for life. Humans depend upon voice recognition to a much greater degree than they probably realize, as evidenced by the instant recognition of a voice on a late, late movie when the face of that now-aged actor has changed beyond instant recognition.

Although the evidence is limited, there are some data that indicate that dolphins can mimic other sounds in both the pulsed sound and whistle modes. One animal, in the pulsed mode, imitated the sound of a brush that was used to clean his tank and, in the whistle mode a constant tone that had been played to it during an experiment. Both of these cases of imitation were spontaneous on the part of that particular dolphin, and the animal was never purposefully rewarded for them.

Visual Communications

Dolphins have better eyesight than was first thought. Experiments indicate that they have good vision both in air and in water. Visual signaling is, therefore, not impossible to the species in either medium, even though the more complex facial signals that mammals such as wolves and primates utilize are not available to dolphins. For speed and maneuverability underwater, the sea-going mammals have also had to sacrifice appendages such as arms, legs, ears, and flexible tail, all of which are capable of conveying so much meaning in terrestrial mammals. But dolphins still retain message-carrying capability in gross movement, body angulations and speed of movement. Threat is conveyed by frontal positioning, open mouth, and arched back. Following Darwin's principle of antithesis, the opposite or submission is indicated by closed mouth and turning the body sideways.

Dolphins are also capable of resolving differences in pigmentation pattern which would allow them to identify species at distances and individuals at close range.

Talking by Touch

Touch is the most intimate of all forms of communication. It is the glue that holds many mammalian societies together. Sexual reproduction and mother-infant relationships are, of course, primarily tactile in nature. Yet tactile communication has received little attention even in our own species. It is only known, for instance, that an infant that receives gentle tactile stimulation has an increased chance of becoming a useful and kindly member of society as well as a good parent, whereas the chances for a neglected or battered child are considerably reduced. In truth, humans are only now coming out of the Puritanical era far enough to admit that tactile communication does indeed exist in their own species.

Touch is used prominently by the Atlantic bottlenosed dolphin. If an infant loses physical contact with the mother, the mother emits several loud whistles and the infant usually returns to her side. If the offspring is feeling too rambunctious and ignores the summons, the mother may lightly punish the offender by holding it down momentarily so that it cannot breathe, or push it, wiggling and squealing, up out of the water for a few seconds. The chastised offender then behaves itself by remaining close to the mother's side.

Adult females swim closely together, touching flippers as they cruise slowly through the water. Such close contact increases as the activity level of the group decreases. This phenomenon is characteristic of many animals that live in groups. As their need for rest and sleep increases, tensions between individuals are reduced, thus bringing the group more closely together just at the time when they do indeed need more group protection. As do most of the primates, dolphins also spend much of their leisure time stroking and nuzzling each other. This type of behavior is obviously well received by the recipient, and again as in the primates, helps to hold a group together.

The application of light punishment suitable to the age of the infant is necessary to their continued well-being. In mammalian societies, this is all part of the socialization process—the learning of the rules under which that society lives. Punishment for infants is gentle, but as the juveniles become larger, breaches of etiquette are taken less lightly by the adults. Blows and bites are inflicted—a form of tactile communication with a meaning that is completely unambiguous.

Can Dolphins Smell or Taste?

Dolphins are not thought to be able to smell, as that part of the brain that processes odor in other mammals is missing in dolphins. Whether or not they are able to detect chemical differences on contact, or "taste," is not fully resolved, but there is subjective reason to believe that they can.

The relatively recent discovery of the interesting sounds made by dolphins and other Cetacea has led to a healthy public interest in these fascinating animals. Most of this interest has centered around two behavioral areas—their communication systems and their intelligence. In view of the number of words that have been written about both, usually attributing enormous capability to dolphins in each area, it will come as a shock to most laymen to learn just how little experimental work has been done with dolphins outside of the area of their echolocation (sonar) system, a subject of considerable interest to the Navy.

There are possibly valid reasons for the limited research and lack of hard data. The cost of working with marine mammals is much higher than comparable projects on rats or birds, for example. Ship time is expensive and maintenance of the animals in captivity is also costly. In actuality, a great vacuum exists in our knowledge of these animals—and where knowledge ends, mythology will certainly take over. It may be many years or never before the American public is willing to support basic research on dolphins. Until such times arrive, loose statements outside of scientific journals as to the intelligence and communicative abilities of dolphins should be viewed with a jaundiced eye. As with all other mythologies, dolphin beliefs may be based on original truth or a rather desperate human need for something a little better and more exciting than is encountered in everyday life.

WHEN PANDAS SCREAM[2]

In December, 1974, the animals in China's Liaoning Province began acting strangely. Hibernating snakes crawled up above ground. Agitated rats appeared in packs. Geese flew wildly. Pigs climbed walls, butted doors and bit off each other's tails. A turtle jumped out of the water and rolled over.

As these and other reports reached local government offices, Chinese geophysicists seemed uncommonly interested in the details of each account. They held meetings, had discussions and, when accounts began to skyrocket, consulted maps and tiltmeters and went in groups to look at well water levels in the province.

At the beginning of February, a series of small seismic waves was felt in the area. Then on February 4, a massive shock wave shook the province and was picked up on seismographs all over the planet. Since China has a long history of quake-caused casualties, a number of countries immediately offered assistance.

But China needed no help. Not only had the Chinese apparently suffered minimal casualties, they had anticipated the quake accurately enough to save perhaps a million lives. Five to ten hours before the quake hit, tens of thousands of people had left their communes, by government directive, and assembled on safe ground.

As scientists elsewhere later learned, the Chinese have a long and abiding respect for the earthquake-sensing abilities of animals. Two years earlier, the government had distributed booklets to all rural families, picturing and describing animals in various states of pre-quake agitation, and directing that any evidence of anomalous animal behavior was to be reported immediately. The 1975 earthquake prediction was a direct result of these instructions.

[2] Article entitled "If Pandas Scream . . . an Earthquake Is Coming," by Phylis Magida, a Chicago freelance writer specializing in food and natural science. *International Wildlife*. 7:36–9. S. '77. Copyright 1977 by the National Wildlife Federation. Reprinted from the September–October issue of *International Wildlife* Magazine.

Actually, a belief in animal prescience is part of many cultures. And creatures in quake-prone places have been credited with powers of prognostication for over 25 centuries. But the total amount of earthquake lore is small compared with the mass of weather lore, which spans several ages and dozens of countries—all using animals to forecast the weather. If swallows flew low or cows looked skyward, to the Holy Romans it meant showers. If horses yawned or roosters crowed, in Finland it meant upcoming drizzles. When flies bit eagerly or fish broke water, when donkeys brayed or sea birds roosted, to early Americans it meant a rain storm was on the way.

Not all the lore was associated with short-term weather changes. In fact, animals were thought to accommodate themselves physically to freezing winters several months in advance. Geese were said to fly south early, turkeys to grow thicker feathers, bears to gluttonize and sport thicker coats, partridges to sprout toe feathers, squirrels to nut excessively—all of these in sympathetic advance rapport with the cold of the oncoming winter.

Zoologists have attempted to explain the lore by pointing out that each species is finely tuned to its own climate and weather—with special adaptations for survival. Every animal evolved in such intimate rapport with its environment that the relationship could almost be called mutual. Recent discoveries, for instance, show that some animals possess senses so extraordinary they seem *extra*sensory. Bats hear ultrasonic rings around us, with a range of hearing five times higher than a human's. Moles have such a sharp sense of distant touch that they reportedly know by the "feel" of the air when a trap has been placed in their burrows. The male emperor moth can sometimes detect a female three miles downwind.

Even more astonishing are the discoveries of animal senses for which there are no human equivalents. Certain fish, such as skates and rays, hunt and navigate by emitting streams of faint electric impulses. Some snakes, including copperheads and rattlers, have a temperature sense of such uncanny accuracy that they coil and strike in response to the warmth they feel coming from their prey.

Not all scientists accept this supersensory explanation for how some animals can "predict" weather. In fact, many weather specialists—the people responsible for inventing the radar storm detector and the automatic weather station— are certain that animals cannot predict weather. At best, they insist, animals merely respond to immediate stimuli, just as crickets chirp in proportion to the ambient warmth.

Thus, the argument goes, swallows fly low before storms because the insects they seek are heavy with pre-storm humidity and have themselves been forced downward. Gulls roost more because pre-storm pressure makes it harder to fly. Fleas bite to excess when pre-rain humidity and pressure release body scents to them. Dogs, donkeys and other animals react to air pressure drops with restlessness and vocalizing. Thick animal coats or early bird migration reflect an ample or deficient food supply in the present, rather than an unusually cold winter on the way.

No matter how their actions are interpreted, animals do behave in diverse ways before storms or frosts. Before earthquakes, however, they all tend to behave in more or less the *same* way. Some scientists call it "restlessness," but laymen might call it *panic*. Before a 373 B.C. quake in Italy, mice, moles and weasels came out of the ground in swarms. Before an 1868 quake in Chile, masses of sea birds cried and flew hysterically inland. Before a 1969 quake in China, zoo keepers reported that the tigers were depressed, the yak had rolled over and refused to eat and the pandas had held their heads and "screamed."

"But what is the basis for this remarkable instinct of animals, reptiles, birds and fish?" one scientist asked as early as 1909 in an issue of *Scientific American.*

At a recent U.S. Geological Survey conference, scientists, considering some pre-quake signals that animals might be responding to, came up with such things as changes in air pressure, in the electric field, in gases exhaled from the ground, in electrostatic charging of aerosol particles, in infra or ultra sound and in the magnetic field. What's interesting is that such changes are present in the upper atmosphere, too, in advance of certain weather.

One theory, that animals might be picking up low-frequency sound prior to rains or quakes, has even been used in weather forecasting in Japan, according to Donald E. Carr, author and scientist. "Gulls, dolphins and jellyfish have long been known to take refuge before the actual approach of a storm; the theory is that they're responding to sounds arising from the pressure of sea waves against air, which are *lower* than the human ear can detect." But so far, no single quake or storm precursor has been found that can elicit response from *every* species.

Based on the little we know about interspecific communication, though, it's possible that a few animals are picking up early signals and telling many others—like the old Tarzan movies where oncoming danger was barked and chirruped in advance through the forest. Perhaps the African rhino birds are telling the rhinos, who're telling the baboons, who're telling the chimps, who're telling the zebras, who're telling the waterbuck, the wildebeest and everything else.

Of course, it's also possible that animals are not sensing anything in advance. Helena C. Kraemer, associate professor of biostatistics at Stanford University, says: "We're not even sure at this point that the animals can predict oncoming quakes; so it's premature to speculate about the physical phenomena to which they might be reacting. What needs to be done is to establish multiple animal monitors at places along major faults."

In fact, the geophysical community in America *has* begun testing animal behavior before earthquakes. Several months ago, Kraemer and other scientists, while monitoring some caged chimpanzees for maturational behavior changes, noted retrospectively on the computer tapes that the chimps had acted restless before some minor quakes near the San Andreas fault. Besides these continuing studies, some pocket mice and kangaroo rats have been placed in monitored stations along the Palmdale Bulge, a section of earth in Southern California which has begun to bulge.

A third study has been established along the San Andreas fault, where geophysicist Ruth Simon, who has studied animals and quakes since 1972, has set up cockroaches in three carefully monitored stations. "It's important to check out every possibility in predicting earthquakes," she says, "since no single geophysical instrument can predict a quake in advance. Even in combination, our instruments don't do better. Animals, though, have the potential of acting as accurate geo-sensors to detect earthquakes before they occur."

But the Chinese do not claim that animals are infallible quake predictors. In 1973, thousands of people were evacuated in freezing weather, in advance of an earthquake that never came. And last year, the deadliest earthquake in four centuries struck Tangshan City 100 miles from Peking, apparently killing at least 655,000 people. Unusual behavior was reported for 33 species of animals before the quake—but not in time enough for a warning to be issued.

The Russians announced in 1969 that they, too, were establishing some animal warning centers in quake-prone areas of the U.S.S.R. Observers there watch the behavior of certain animals for "disaster sensitivity." According to one Soviet geophysicist, animals, once you can read them, "are the most sensitive disaster barometers known to science."

In America, the geophysical community wants to find out what the animals are sensing so that they can build an instrument to duplicate it, but this may be more difficult than it sounds. Scientists have suggested that, from one perspective, all of our tools and machines—whether barometers or seismographs—can be viewed as mechanical attempts to duplicate those senses that the animals possess. Our sonar, for example, which is so heavy and which we think so splendid, is actually amateurish in comparison with that of a bat, whose own sonar weighs less than one half ounce, and which his ancestors invented several million years ago.

IN SEA RESCUES, THE EAGLE EYES
ARE PIGEONS[3]

The Coast Guard intends to spend $146,000 over the next two years to train a "rescue squab" of pigeons to find people lost at sea.

A Navy report just released says that in experiments, pigeons strapped on a helicopter outdid Coast Guard air crews every time in spotting objects tossing on the ocean's surface.

But, in the first flight casualty of its kind, the first three pigeon graduates drowned at sea when the helicopter they were riding in ran out of fuel and crash-landed off Hawaii. The humans got out unscathed.

The Coast Guard is paying the Navy to train 10 more pigeons for rescue duty as part of Project Sea Hunt.

These pigeons will be better protected on their air rescue missions, Douglas Conley, Coast Guard project officer, said in an interview yesterday.

Instead of riding in a plastic bubble underneath the helicopter, as was the case in the fateful February crash, the pigeons will ride in a capsule on the side of the helicopter, Conley said. The earlier capsule tore off and sank when the helicopter crash-landed. The three pigeons inside, strapped to their special couches, drowned.

Before being lost at sea, the pigeons piled up an impressive record in search and rescue drills over the Pacific. Some evidence from the Naval ocean Systems Center report on the competition between pigeons and humans:

—The pigeons spotted the floating target, colored life preserver orange, 90 percent of the time on the helicopter's first pass while the air crew saw the object only 38 percent of the time. (The pigeons pecked, as they were trained ashore to do, on a special pedal that flashed a signal to the pilot.)

—The pigeons outperformed the human spotters even

[3] Article by George C. Wilson, staff writer. Washington *Post*. p A1.Jl. 31, '79 © The Washington *Post*. Reprinted with permission.

though the "aircraft personnel had prior knowledge of the target's approximate position and could relax between trials."

—Besides spotting the object in 80 of 89 trials while the humans did not see it at all on 55 of those first passes, the pigeons also were the first to report the sighting almost every time.

"Those pigeons really did well," Conley said. He predicted the new class will see duty with several of the Coast Guard's 12 air rescue stations.

The 10 pigeons attending ground school at the Navy's laboratory on Kailua, Hawaii, are expected to be ready for flight duty in October [1979].

In the first part of ground school, the pigeons are taught to peck a lever every time they are shown orange—the color of life preservers. They are rewarded with food if they peck at the right instant.

After mastering pecking, the pigeons are subjected to the noises a helicopter makes so they will not be frightened when they fly in one.

As their training progresses, the pigeons are strapped into special tiny couches, in a capsule and taken to a spot where they can look out to sea. Orange objects are towed out to sea to test the pigeons' acuity and response time.

All this training takes about six months. Conley said yesterday that some of the new class of pigeons probably will "wash out," but he hopes at least six of them will qualify for helicopter duty.

The six pigeons which have an average life span of 10 years would give the Coast Guard two crews for search and rescue. Each capsule carries three pigeons in separate compartments facing different directions to cover all points of the compass in searching the sea for orange life preservers.

If all goes well, Conley said, the pigeons eventually will be trained to peck their signal pedals when they see yellow or red as well as orange. Some life preservers are those colors.

Asked why the Coast Guard did not train hawks or falcons for sharp-eyed searching of the sea, Conley said "plain old park pigeons" also see well and are easier to train "probably because they're calmer. They don't seem to mind it."

IN THIS ZOO, VISITORS LEARN, THOUGH NO MORE THAN ANIMALS[4]

A light flashes on, high against the back wall of the 30-foot cage, and a young diana monkey—a small, elegant creature with black fur and a white beard—climbs a network of steel exercise bars to reach it. The monkey pulls a chain beside the light, and another light flashes on at the right end of the cage. A female monkey, the mother of the young one, pulls a chain beside that light, and receives a blue token, like a large plastic poker chip, from a slot in the wall. She reaches out and drops the token ten feet to the concrete floor. The little monkey climbs down, picks up the token and carries it to the lower left-hand corner of the wall where there are two openings. He drops the token into one opening, and two pieces of apple emerge from the other. Before he can take the apple, though, his mother—who has never learned to put the token into the slot—comes over and grabs most of it away from him.

A man holding a small child in his arms is standing in a crowd of zoo visitors watching the monkeys. The child, restless, begins to cry and fuss. "Be quiet," the man snaps. "I want to see this."

Someone puts a dime in a coin slot in front of the cage. The first light flashes on again. Again, the little monkey climbs up and pulls the chain. Again, his mother collects the token and drops it on the floor. This time, though, when the little monkey picks it up, he saunters around the cage with it, pretending the vending machine in the corner is the farthest thing from his mind. He walks slowly along a long bar at right angles to the wall. He sits on a short bar beside his sibling. He

[4] Article by Daniel Jack Chasan, author of several articles for *Smithsonian*. *Smithsonian*. 5:22–9. Jl. '74. © Smithsonian Institution 1974. All rights reserved. Reproduction in whole or in part without permission is prohibited. Reprinted with permission.

does everything but whistle. Finally, he makes his move toward the slot. This time, his mother stays by the second light, and his sibling tries to rip off the pieces of apple.

The diana monkeys' initiation into the world of specie payment, coin vending machines and deferred rewards is only one part—although admittedly a spectacular one—of a unique research program that has been going on at the zoo in Portland, Oregon, since 1972. The Portland Zoological Gardens consist of a modest collection of drab concrete buildings amid Douglas firs in the hilly outskirts of the city. It is not a large zoo, and it is hovering on the brink of insolvency; even now, it depends on the labor of young volunteers. Yet its research program is one of the most striking recent innovations in the world of zoos.

In addition to the diana monkeys, the cast of characters includes gibbons that have also learned to pull levers when lights come on, chimps that are learning the standard American Sign Language for the deaf and mute, and an assortment of seals, ostriches, giraffes, camels and elephants that have learned to press lighted panels with their noses, beaks, chins and trunks, all in exchange for food. The animals all get fed every day whether or not they choose to cooperate with the experiments. But evidently not even animals live by bread alone: They virtually always do cooperate without any twisting of arms, legs or flippers. In fact, when the gibbons' apparatus was shut off so that the zoo could equip it with solid-state circuits, gibbons holding food in their hands would climb up and pull the useless chains, trying to get a little action. In the near future, they may be joined by orangutans that play ticktacktoe against human opponents, and by servals—small, spotted African cats capable of catching birds on the wing—that leap for fast-moving targets whizzing by on overhead tracks.

The human beings who set these processes up want to see how fast the various animals can learn them, how fast the animals can learn to make "reversals" (for example, hit an unlighted panel instead of a lighted one), and how the processes affect social interactions among the animals involved. They also want to give the animals some task—preferably something similar to what they would do in the wild—to counteract the boredom of a traditional zoo existence.

Zoo directors in other cities tend to think all this will be good for both the animals and the public, but the feelings of Portland's citizens have been decidedly mixed. Not that anyone objects to seeing the animals at work. But "operant conditioning" and the other professional jargon used to describe what is going on fills some people with discomfiting visions of 1984. And some people, amazingly, seem offended by the very idea of a zoo engaging in research. At least one local politician has been known to argue that the public supports the zoo and the public should be entertained by it, period.

The idea of a zoo as pure entertainment receives short shrift from Portland's director, a tall, assertive man with graying muttonchop whiskers and an extracurricular interest in fine wines, named Philip Ogilvie. Ogilvie, who began his career as an academic biologist specializing in chameleons, came to Portland three years ago after directing a zoo in Oklahoma City and designing the (soon to be built) Minnesota Zoological Garden. "Behavioral engineering"—in this case teaching the various creatures to do something in exchange for their food—is at the core of his program in Portland. And he has pushed hard to establish it. "We'd like to set up something like that, too, if we had the money," a progressive zoo director in another city said recently. Then he thought a moment and conceded, "Hell, Phil didn't have the money, either. He just scraped it together from here and there."

Simply amusing the populace might have been easier but, Ogilvie says, public entertainment "doesn't justify taking animals out of the wild." Asked if anything really does justify taking animals out of the wild, he laughs. "I wonder about that," he says. "Sometimes I'm not sure anything does. *If* anything does, it's interpreting their behavior to the public."

Since the rise of the environmental movement, many younger zoo directors have drawn a sense of purpose from the idea that they can make people aware of the interrelatedness of all living things, and the importance of preserving animal life not directly useful to human beings. Ogilvie is basically of this school. But he quickly points out that, unlike many latter-day environmentalists, he was teaching ecology as a college subject years before it became a topic of general concern or a rationale for the operation of zoos. And he is skeptical of the idea of zoos as breeding places for animal species that have become endangered in the wild. He says, succinctly, that "Preserving a small group of animals while their habitat is destroyed is nonsense. If the habitat goes, that's it." He does hope, though, that by demonstrating that an animal doesn't exist in a vacuum, the Portland exhibits will help persuade people that habitats should be preserved.

Whatever the Portland exhibits teach or fail to teach the zoo-going public, both Ogilvie and Hal Markowitz, his research director, are dead certain that they make life much more interesting for the animals involved. Both men are convinced that subjecting an intelligent animal to traditional zoo life—spending most of its hours on a concrete cage floor onto which its food arrives with a splat once a day—verges on sadism. "If you set out to design an environment of total sensory deprivation," Ogilvie says, "you couldn't do much better than a traditional zoo cage." That seemed obvious to Ogilvie when he first became a zoo director in 1965 (after reading in a newspaper that the Oklahoma City Zoo had an opening), and it seemed obvious to Markowitz when the Zoological Society appointed him as the Portland zoo's director of research in 1972. (Markowitz, a specialist in brain chemistry and function, had been chairman of the psychology department at nearby Pacific University.)

When Markowitz arrived at the zoo, he first turned his attention to the gibbons because, he has written, for gibbons the "routine feeding procedure seemed especially grotesque. Watching tree-dwelling animals sit on the cement and awkwardly pick at piles of food took much of the joy out of visits to these handsome apes." His idea was to give the gibbons something to do that would involve as much swinging by their hands as possible, and would do it within the confines of their existing 30-foot cage. There were two openings with ledges already built into the back of the cage, high up on the wall, so Markowitz designed a system in which lights and levers were installed at both openings. If a visitor drops a coin into a box outside the cage, the light at the left flashes on. (If no one puts in a coin, a clock will operate the light after a while anyway.) When the gibbon pulls the lever beside that light, the light at the right end of the cage flashes on. When a gibbon pulls the lever beside that one, a piece of food emerges from a slot in the wall.

Harvey Catches on Fast

A young male known as Harvey Wallbanger quickly established himself as the main puller of the first lever, and at first found himself being exploited by his cage mates, who would simply sit by the food slot, waiting to pull the second lever and help themselves as soon as he pulled the first. Harvey caught on fast, though, and although he doesn't object to feeding his old mother, he now will operate the first lever only if his brother stands far enough away from the food slot to give Harvey a fair chance of beating him to the second.

Markowitz' most elaborate experiments have all involved primates, but nonprimates have got something close to equal time. Markowitz and his associates have, after all, "done" elephants and seals. They have done ostriches and giraffes. They have done camels. Camels?

"No one has ever done research with camels before," Markowitz explains. "Besides, I *like* camels." The camels' apparatus consists of a microswitch and a food slot, designed so that if a camel hits the switch the requisite number of times, it gets food through the slot. The idea was to see how many times the camel would be willing to hit the switch with its nose to get a single reward. At what point would the animal decide that the reward wasn't worth the effort? The trouble was, the camel didn't use its nose; contrary to all expectations, it walked up to the machine, put its chin against the switch, and began vibrating its chin so rapidly that it quickly hit the switch dozens of times with virtually no effort. Vic

Stevens, the designer, had expected the camel to give out while the repetitions were still in double figures. Instead, it began to show substantial strain only when it hit 150. The experiment is still going on, but now it is organized somewhat more on the camel's terms.

The elephants also have proved to be remarkable subjects. A Reed College psychology professor named Les Squier had taught the zoo's elephants to press lighted panels with their trunks in exchange for food in 1965. Squier had quickly abandoned the project, though, and the elephants hadn't even seen the apparatus again until zoo employees found it on a scrap heap in 1973. They fixed it up and wheeled it into the elephant house, where, to everyone's astonishment, a Vietnamese elephant named Tuy Hoa began working it as if she had been practicing all along. It seems an elephant really doesn't forget. Tuy Hoa's cage mates, Rosy and Belle, had a lot of trouble with the apparatus, but medical examinations later showed that it was their eyesight, not their memories, that had dimmed.

If it is tempting to anthropomorphize with the elephants or dianas, it is absolutely unavoidable with the chimps, who are, after all, being taught a human language (albeit one of signs or gestures rather than vocables). The chimps are being educated by a group of volunteers headed by Katheryne Johnson, a dark-haired young woman whose manner conveys both energy and calm—qualities which are evidently much needed when working with chimpanzees. She sits very still while they run and wrestle around her, but when they're on her lap and ready to work, she is busy every second, talking to them, showing them signs, guiding their hands into the proper positions, rewarding them with drinks of juice and pieces of fruit. Her efforts have paid off: Two young chimps named Charlie and Jezebel have each mastered more than two dozen words, and are quite capable of asking to be fed, tickled or picked up, or referring to apples, oranges or bananas by sign name. Not long ago, the chimps were first seen talking to each other in sign language. Katheryne Johnson had been playing a chase game with Charlie. After a while she got tired and stopped. Charlie made the sign for "chase" to Jezebel, and she took off with him after her in hot pursuit.

The people who work with chimps are clearly crazy about the animals, and more interested in the chimps' own linguistic progress than in the possibility of their communicating with the public at large. For Ogilvie, even the chimps' linguistic progress isn't the most important thing. He explains that teaching the chimps sign language is only a part, and not an indispensable one, of an effort to find out if an "enriched" environment does them any observable good. He wants eventually to have observations made of Portland's chimps, a group of chimps from a traditional zoo, a group of chimps from a circus or carnival ("who receive a lot of *negative* reinforcement" in the course of their training) and a group of wild chimps. The point will be to see which of the first three groups behaves most like the wild chimps, who presumably qualify as a desirable norm. Ogilvie says he expects both the Portland chimps and the circus chimps to behave more like their wild relatives than the traditional zoo chimps do, but expects little difference between the two. "I suspect," he says, "that, in terms of chimp behavior, it doesn't matter whether the reinforcement is positive or negative; the important thing is interaction."

People have tried "enriching" chimps' environments before, and have even taught them the American Sign Language—Beatrice T. and R. Allen Gardner, in Reno, Nevada, have been teaching ASL [American Sign Language] to a chimp named Washoe since 1966, and William B. Lemmon, in Norman, Oklahoma (an old friend and colleague of Ogilvie), has been teaching ASL to chimps, too—but no one has ever done it in a zoo before.

Ogilvie and Markowitz have been surprised by how quickly the animals learn. Markowitz says that everyone has overestimated the time it would take for virtually all the animals to master their equipment. Even the ostriches—big, surly birds that the keepers give a wide berth to and that no one has ever credited with much intelligence—have learned to peck a single key faster than anyone expected. The whole ostrich colony now looks quite expert as it stands in front of its apparatus, each bird in turn pecking open-beaked with a movement of its long, snaky neck, then reaching down for its reward. The birds were so fond of peanuts, their original reward, and so adept at getting them that they ate virtually nothing else and single-handedly unbalanced their own diets.

What is the scientific significance of doing this or any other kind of behavioral research in a zoo? Markowitz explains that laboratory animals are virtually always studied in isolation, which is most unnatural for the animals and which "may be a great distortion." In the zoo, a researcher can—in fact, a researcher pretty well must—study animals in a social context, surrounded by their peers. This does not make for neat experiments, but it may make for valuable results.

The researcher may also get a chance to function in a social context, himself. A case in point is a recent visit by Markowitz to the diana monkeys' cage. As Markowitz walks up to the cage, a young woman in a green jacket, accompanied by her husband and a horde of small children, is jumping up and down in front of the glass. The top light is shining in the cage, and the female monkey is sitting near it. As the woman jumps, her dark hair swinging behind her, she yells to the monkey, "Pull it. Pull it. Pull the chain." Then she turns to Markowitz, who is standing there in a white lab coat, and complains, "He won't pull it."

"*She* never does," Markowitz tells her with quiet authority. Perversely, the monkey pulls the chain. The male diana pulls the second chain and gets the token. He climbs down to the food slot, where he rummages around like a kid hoping to find something in a coin return. He doesn't insert the token. Since the monkeys have already obtained food 84 times that day, it's not hard to see why he doesn't.

But the woman in the green jacket isn't sympathetic. She tries to move the monkey toward the slot with body English. She jumps up and down again. "Put it in the slot," she yells. *"Put it in the slot, you dummy!"*

Markowitz' experiment has obviously struck a responsive

chord. He smiles. "Well," he says, "this is the most reinforce-ment *I've* gotten in months."

MONKEY RESEARCH APPLIED TO MAN[5]

The light was just coming up behind Salt Pond [St. Kitts, West Indies] as Laura Frankl wriggled out of her sleeping bag, shook out her boots and made her way through the shoul-der-high grass.

Concealing herself in a natural blind near the water's edge, she remained quiet and motionless for the next hour. Suddenly she raised her field glasses and nudged her compan-ion. "There," she whispered.

Scarcely 150 yards away, two wild monkeys had emerged from the dense growth of Whaleback Hill and were leading their troop across the sandbar spanning the pond to their feeding grounds. Two playful juveniles tumbled over each other, silhouetted against the gleaming water. A venerable male who had lingered to nibble an acacia thorn bush now followed, standing up on his hindlegs to look back every so often. A fifth brought up the rear.

It was a magic moment for Frankl, an 18-year-old sopho-more in biology from Occidental College in Los Angeles, whose expedition until now had caught only glimpses of these elusive animals.

She is one of about 30 U.S. students and scientists who were on the island last summer, attracted by the prospect of seeing and studying these close relatives of man in the wild, at what locals call "the monkey farm."

Quite possibly the most unusual research facility in the world, the Behavioral Sciences Foundation is headquartered at Estridge, an old plantation just 16 miles from where Frankl spotted her monkeys. It coordinates a host of projects in psy-chiatry, anthropology and archeology, and uses the monkey

[5] Article entitled "Students Take to the Wild in Search of Man's Closest Relatives," by Lois Timnick, journalist, Los Angeles *Times*. Washington *Post*. p M15. Ap. 22, '79. © Copyright The Los Angeles Times Company. Reprinted with permission.

to study such human concerns as aggression, stress and anxiety, leadership, sex differences, depression, drug addiction and brain damage.

One morning at the monkey farm, for example, Yale University psychiatrist Gene Redmond was already bent over an anesthetized animal. He wanted to remove five monkey brains for analysis that day, and the lab, which is not air conditioned, already was sweltering.

Outside, from a rickety observation tower in the trees, University of California, Davis, anthropology student Janet Franklin looked down on a troop of 33 monkeys, recording their behavior on a long score sheet.

At the edge of the southeast peninsula's remote Great Salt Pond, University of California, Los Angeles, graduate student archeologist Doug Armstrong, 23, and 17-year-old Ralph Black of Bethesda picked up the first of the numerous fragments of pottery, shell and rock tools—4,000 years old, perhaps—they'd find that day in this uninhabited area of scrub and savanna.

And Jeff Lannery, director of a primatology summer school program at Estridge, had long finished taking monkey blood samples and was now talking with UCLA psychiatrist Frank Ervin, the man behind all this activity.

The laboratory is housed in the former slave quarters and outdoor kitchen—a whitewashed stone building with red shutters and a corrugated metal roof—of the plantation. Ants scurry across the wooden work tables.

The electric current is such that the refrigerated centrifuge can either refrigerate or centrifuge but not both—so specimens are first cooled, then the compressor motor is turned off and the centrifuge is switched on.

Frozen monkeys and ice cream share space in the noisy freezer (even though it's clearly marked "no food") across the way in the old Great House.

The water often does not run. And the heat—it is unbearably humid and sometimes into the high 90s by midmorning—dictates that the sweaty scientists perform their delicate experimental surgery stripped to the waist.

But the primitiveness of the setting is matched by the excitement of those who come here to work, lured by the abundance of an animal the locals consider an agricultural pest—the green monkey or vervet, known scientifically as *Cercopithecus aethiops sabaeus*. This is a species of Old World monkey millions of years closer to man than the New World variety and found on this continent only on the Caribbean Islands of St. Kitts, Nevis and Barbados.

Today there is a monkey shortage elsewhere, but there are an estimated 30,000 vervets on the 68-square-mile island, 150 of them in captivity at Estridge. Some are trapped and sold to make polio vaccine; others have been sent to the Sepulveda VA Hospital at Los Angeles and to Mexico and Cuba to establish troops of monkeys there.

The island provides a cheap and plentiful supply of research subjects closely related to man and with similar genetic variability. And it offers scientists the opportunity to observe them in social groups either at close range in two large enclosures at Estridge, or in the wild in three very different environments—the tropical rain forest of Mt. Misery, a volcanic crater; the ravines bordering the sugar cane fields; and the savanna and slopes of the southeast peninsula.

Some of the research centers on how animals develop normally—for example, the differences in how young males and females play and whether those differences have anything to do with their role as adults. These animals are only watched, not interfered with or experimented on in any way.

A second type of research at Estridge is assessing the effects—on groups of normal animals—of brain-altering drugs or environmental changes like crowding or separation. And a third type of study consists of damaging some animals—making them "crazy" or violent, for example—and then trying to find ways of reversing that damage. A small percentage of the animals must be killed—the scientists call it "sacrificing"—to gain direct knowledge of what is happening in the brain.

The animals are usually studied in groups, an aspect largely ignored in biological research, even though a monkey—or a person—may react differently to a drug or even brain damage in isolation than in a social situation.

The consequences of specific brain damage, for example,

differ, depending on the animal's social role. Scientific director Mike Raleigh, also of UCLA, and Dieter Steklis of Rutgers did identical brain surgery on nine vervets in a group of 21 they'd been watching carefully for five months. They removed a tiny piece of tissue from a part of the frontal cortex thought to be associated with emotion and mood, then put the monkeys back with the troop and watched them for the next six months.

All of the brain-damaged animals became less aggressive, huddled with a new set of friends and spent more time alone—as expected. But how much and in what ways they were changed depended largely on their age and sex and rank and how the other monkeys reacted to them.

The adult males' success at one-to-one fighting dropped, limiting their access to females, food and shelter. The females quit grooming and huddling and no longer came to their sisters' aid during fights. The young played less. Young females lost interest in taking care of the infants.

Formerly high-ranking males were devastated if a normal male challenged them, but started getting better at sex and grooming and fighting if the rival was removed for a week or so. Changing the environment didn't help the damaged females much.

The normal monkeys either ignored their brain-damaged brothers or continually harassed them, depending on whether they'd been competitors before. And they often compensated for the damaged monkeys' deficits, say, by more grooming of a neglected infant.

Ervin and his colleagues have methodically watched their captives for four years now and feel they can describe with confidence how the troop functions; who does what to whom and how frequently and when.

Now they are in a position to either make physical changes in the animals (via drugs or surgery) and see what changes in behavior result, or manipulate the social setting and measure any resulting biological changes—in hormones and other substances in the blood and brain.

One recent project, for example, involved raising and lowering serotonin levels, a brain chemical implicated in sleep and sex behaviors and certain kinds of depression. Raleigh, Ervin and Flannery administered drugs to 45 animals, causing them to make more or less serotonin, and looked at the behavioral consequences. In general, the animals with elevated serotonin were mellower, quieter, friendlier; those with lowered serotonin became more irritable.

Now the team plans to do just the opposite: to manipulate behavior—say, by separating juveniles who have become attached to each other through playing and growing up together, thus creating a sort of experimental "depression"—and then measure any changes in brain chemicals.

What happens in a monkey may not necessarily happen in man. But because these St. Kitts monkeys are, except for the great apes, our nearest kin, the result of these kinds of studies are bound to be more relevant to human problems than behavioral studies based on rats or mice, Ervin says.

At 52, he is one of the United States' most renowned electro-physiologists and an expert on violence and the brain.

Much of the research behind his surprising report of an abnormal peptide found in the blood of schizophrenic patients last year was carried out at the monkey farm. (The substance, isolated from waste fluid saved from schizophrenic patients undergoing experimental kidney dialysis, was injected into monkeys. At high doses it caused convulsions and death: at lower levels it caused convulsive patterns in brain wave tracings, indicating that it was exciting the brain's limbic system, the region thought to be involved in emotional disturbances).

BEHAVIOR MOD, DOWN ON THE FARM[6]

He comes on stage purposefully, turns to his glittery piano and, after flipping his white tails, plays a striking series of ar-

[6] Article originally titled "Can a Chicken Play Poker?" by Beth Nissen, contributing journalist, The Wall Street Journal. Washington Post. p B1. F. 20, '79. Reprinted by permission of The Wall Street Journal, © Dow Jones & Company, Inc., 1979. All rights reserved.

peggios. To delighted applause, he ducks back into the wings.

He is, in fact, a duck—trained here by Animal Behavior Enterprises Inc., a small organization of biologists and technicians that can control the actions of animals as large as whales and as small as cockroaches with behavior modification.

At the company's noisy 25-acre farm in central Arkansas, parrots rollerskate, racoons play basketball, bunnies run roulette wheels, and chickens do card tricks. "We can train any animal to do anything within its physical limits," says Marian Breland Bailey, who founded Animal Behavior Enterprises with her late husband, Keller Breland, in 1947. Since then she has helped train more than 8,000 animals from almost 200 species—including turkeys, dolphins, cows, snakes and reindeer.

To make research and animal training economically feasible, the organization uses its trained animals commercially for entertainment—leasing them to shopping malls and fairs for coin-operated shows and exhibiting them at Animal Wonderland and the I.Q. Zoo, the company's own tourist attractions in Hot Springs.

Animal Behavior's training technique, which is approved by the American Humane Association, strengthens and then controls part of an animal's natural random behavior—say, a chicken's pecking—by immediate positive reinforcement. If reinforcement is consistent, the desired behavior is likely to be performed again and with increased frequency, and eventually on command.

To show how foolproof the technique is, Bailey has this reporter train a chicken, the animal used most often by Animal Behavior Enterprises in its trained acts. "If you can train a chicken, you can train anything," says Bailey, a tiny, white-haired woman whom everyone rather aptly calls "Mouse."

I am to teach my common barnyard hen ("If she wasn't here, she'd be stew," says one trainer) to pick a winning poker hand by pecking a card marked with a black dot. I have a hand-held button connected to an automatic feeder; when I press it, there is a dull bang and bits of grain fall to a feed tray. The chicken is first conditioned to run to the feeder and eat at the sound of the bang.

"At the beginning of training, reinforce the animal for even a good try at the desired behavior," instructs Bailey. My chicken struts around a bit before she finally gives the eagle eye to the three cards I'm holding. Bang, I reinforce her for looking in the right place. On her next try, she comes close and takes an inquisitive peck at my hand. Bang, I reinforce the pecking action. She pecks a card, any card. Bang, I again reinforce the correct action.

The hen is thereafter reinforced only for pecking the marked card, until, after two hours, she has become an unerring cardsharp. Mastering the training of this barnyard animal carries a special satisfaction for me. At the Texas State Fair last summer, another chicken from Hot Springs dealt me a humiliating defeat in tic-tac-toe.

Once trained, the animals never "forget" the correct response. "You can take Burt Backquack, the piano-playing duck, away from his piano for two years and he'll still remember what to do," says Bailey. "There just aren't that many pianos in the life of a duck."

Most of the animals are reinforced with food, because hunger is the easiest natural drive to work with. (Animals are never starved; the "reward" food is part of their daily ration.) Higher animals like dogs and horses will respond to social reinforcement—pats, hugs, and words spoken in a kind tone. Company trainers even used darkness as a reinforcement when they were training a cockroach to pull a lever.

Applying knowledge of different species and their habits—such as the cockroach's love of darkness—was the Brelands' own contribution to the successful training technique. They also drew from the work of Ivan Pavlov (who, with his salivating dog, originated the conditioned-reflex theory) and from psychologist B. F. Skinner's studies of conditioned response.

Keller and Marian Breland, both psychologists, began their animal behavior studies with Skinner at the University of Minnesota in the early 1940s. In 1941, they joined him in work on his war research project—a pigeon-guided missile system.

The idea was to have a pigeon keep a missile on target by pecking rapidly at an image of the target on a cross-hair screen. Once trained, the sharp-eyed pigeons were almost infallible, even when tipped, gyrated and drugged. Nevertheless, the project was dropped.

"The pigeons did exactly what they were supposed to do," says Robert Bailey, the company's staff biologist and now Marian Bailey's husband. "But let's just say the military lacked faith."

The pigeon project, however, secured the Brelands' faith in B. F. Skinner's animal-behavior work. "They took my theory, applied it well enough to make a living from it and, in the process, had all sorts of useful accidents which we've all learned from," says Skinner, who is retired from his psychology post at Harvard University. The Brelands started their business by training animals for advertising and built it up by doing animal-behavior experiments for the government, most of which are still classified.

One declassified project, field-tested by the Army for use in Vietnam, was an ambush-detection system in which trained pigeons would fly ahead of a convoy and watch for concealed humans. Each pigeon carried a small transmitter that emitted a steady signal as the bird flew. The pigeon was trained to land if it saw anyone lying, kneeling or hiding off the road; when it landed, the signal stopped and the troops were warned.

Animal Behavior Enterprises, which did about $500,000 in business in 1977, stopped all work for the government last year but is still asked to do extraordinary animal training. The Baileys refused a recent request from a Lion Country Safari executive in California who wanted them to train a bull elephant to charge visitors but stop just short of the touring car. "We felt there would be safer ways to startle people," Robert Bailey explains. They also turned down a man who, for unknown reasons, asked them to teach his donkey to smile.

In addition to wanting to train untried species, the Baileys would like to train animals already in zoos and nature parks to do, on cue, what they do in nature. "We could, for example, train a raccoon to go to a pond and get a crayfish," explains Marian Bailey, "or we could train a bear to hit at something with all his might. People could see the animal in action instead of just lying in the corner of its cage."

So far, zoos have been wary of the idea, even though the Baileys say the natural-behavior exhibits could be made coin-operated.

EDITOR'S INTRODUCTION

This section concentrates on articles that deal with the commercial use and exploitation of animals by humans.

First is an article by Sam Bleecker originally published in *Harper's*. It is a concise catalog of the amazing number of products we make from just a single species of animal—in this case, the cow, from which we get food, leather, chewing gum, fertilizer, insulin, glycerin, to name only a few items in Mr. Bleecker's list. Next, "The Beastly Harvest," written by Margot Hornblower, a staff reporter for the Washington *Post*, investigates the ever-increasing illegal traffic in endangered species all over the world and makes the case that animal smuggling raises issues that reach far beyond conservation.

As consumer demand is the main impetus in sustaining the inhumane and illegal trade in animals, it is also the motivation behind the attempt by a large-scale major utility corporation to engage in fish culture. Anthony S. Policastro, who has often written on maritime matters, reports in the *News Tribune* on the attempt to combine animal husbandry with advanced technology, thereby realizing high yield and product marketability. High yield was also the aim of two other aquaculture researchers who used backyard swimming pools to raise fish in a scientifically controlled environment. Anthony DeCrosta describes their work in the fourth article from *Organic Farming and Gardening*.

The final article was written by Janet Raloff in *Science News*, and it deals with an emotional issue. She examines in detail the controversial question of whether the killing of baby harp seals in the North Atlantic is an inhumane practice and a matter of exploitation or a necessary concomitant of Canadian national economics.

BIOLOGICAL IMPERIALISM[1]

The phrase "commercial exploitation of animals" has a bad ring to it. Animal lovers find in it the suggestion that cruelty equals profits. Moralists confound it with questions about rights and natural laws. Yet where would we be if not for human enterprise in the refashioning of animal parts and products?

Consider, if you will, just one animal, the steer. A steer is not all steak. Sixteen percent of a steer carcass goes into the production of such useful spinoffs as paper boxes, rubber tires, camera film, case-hardened steel, refined sugar, vitamins, and toothbrush handles. From the steer's fat and hide come glycerin, soap, chewing gum, insulating materials, and oleo, a base used in the manufacture of textile lubricants and margarine. Steer bones, horns, and hooves find their way into sandpaper, wallpaper, violin strings, neat's-foot oil, and fertilizer.

Even more significant are the pharmaceutical uses. Cattle are the source of nearly 400 drugs, many developed within the past decade. Most notable is insulin, which is derived from the pancreas. It requires 60,000 cattle pancreas glands to produce one pound of insulin, or twenty-six steers to keep one diabetic alive for a year. Nationwide, more than 300 million cattle are needed to support the country's 12 million diabetics.

From the steer's lungs comes heparin, an anticoagulant used in the treatment of phlebitis and other circulatory diseases. Adrenal glands are the source of epinephrine, a neurotransmitter used in the treatment of asthma, hay fever, and shock. Adrenal cortex derivatives are used in treating Addison's disease, an often fatal disorder of the human cortex. Cattle thyroid extract is used, like insulin, to supplement the

[1] Article by Samuel E. Bleecker, science journalist and scriptwriter. *Harper's*. 252:4. Mr. '76. Copyright © 1976 by Harper's Magazine. All rights reserved. Reprinted from the March 1976 issue by special permission.

human body's insufficient output. ACTH, the controlling hormone of the pituitary gland, relieves rheumatoid arthritis, rheumatic heart disease, bronchial asthma, acute eye disease, and inflammation of the colon. Rennet, made from the stomach lining of calves, is a mild enzyme that aids digestion when added to infant's milk. It is also a curdling agent used in cheese production.

The list could go on, but the point is made.

THE BEASTLY HARVEST[2]

In a mountainous desert along the Rio Grande a few months ago, US agents arrested five men and seized a million dollars worth of goods smuggled over the Mexican border. The haul: 17,500 lynx, ring-tailed cat, gray fox and other pelts destined for European markets.

Last year, a leading Bogota newspaper exposed a massive underground traffic in endangered crocodile skins, parrots and snakes, smuggled from Colombia through Panama to Europe and Japan. Hugo Torrijos, brother of the former Panamanian leader, was implicated in the trade.

About the same time, six crowded crates of live animals—including leopards, tapirs, 50 baby macaque monkeys and 38 white-handed gibbons—were shipped from Vientiane, Laos, to Brussels. The cargo provoked an international outcry among conservationists because the rare gibbons, a species native to Thailand, could only have been smuggled across the Mekong River.

These three events are not isolated incidents. According to government officials in the United States, Africa, South America and Asia, they are part of a growing international scandal: the illegal traffic in endangered species. While there is a large legal trade in common animals such as mink, the

---

[2] Article by Margot Hornblower, staff writer for The Washington *Post*. Washington *Post Magazine*. p 19+. Jl. 8, '79. © The Washington Post. Reprinted with permission.

growing traffic in endangered species is illegal because it breaks the law of countries where the animals are caught and violates the International Convention on Endangered Flora and Fauna, a treaty signed by 51 nations. The trade in rare plants and animals is a business involving hundreds of millions of dollars, corrupt public officials, "laundered" import documents, physical brutality to animals, and a cast of characters ranging from New Guinea tribesmen to the sophisticated operators of organized crime rings.

"The profits in illegal wildlife are equivalent to profits in the drug trade," says US Justice Department attorney Kenneth Berlin. "For a $1,000 investment, the smuggler can make ten grand."

Rhino horn—ground into powder for its mythical aphrodisiac attributes—brings $600 an ounce in the Far East, twice the price of gold. A woman's crocodile handbag costs $400 in West Germany. A majestic purple parrot known as a hyacinth macaw fetches $5,000 smuggled to the United States from Brazil. An endangered peregrine falcon is worth $10,000 to an Arab sheik.

The trade, coupled with increasing human destruction of jungles and other wildlife habitat, has brought hundreds of species to the edge of extinction: the Asian elephant, the Java rhino, the Bengal tiger, the Mexican green sea turtle, Australia's golden-shouldered parrot, Rwanda's mountain gorilla.

Moreover, the animal trade is a source of tension between Third World and industrialized countries. Africans and South Americans see it as yet another example of wealthy countries exploiting their resources and giving them little in return.

"It's a pretty dirty, sordid business," said Russell Train, president of the World Wildlife Fund. "A few dishonest dealers get rich, but it does not significantly help the economies of the developing countries."

Wildlife trading has probably existed since the stone age, but only recently has it reached the alarming point of devastating whole species. It can be traced, in the familiar pattern of the developing world, to the rise in population. The tribesman who must feed his family from an ever-shrinking resource base sees in ivory an easy profit. And American boom babies, now of age, are greedy for fashion furs and snakeskin sandals.

In 1976, the most recent statistics show, the United States imported 91 million wildlife products. . . . Of course, not all, nor even a majority of these items, are illegal. But US officials are unable to estimate the magnitude of illegal trade. Much of it enters the country with phony documents masquerading as legal. A good deal slips in over the border or through poorly guarded customs ports.

The difficulty is determining what's legal. The same cat's skin may be illegal if it comes from a country which prohibits wildlife exports, or legal if it comes from a nation which encourages trade. And how to tell the difference between a watchband made from an endangered snake or one from a common snake? Between a rare orchid and an everyday variety?

The confusion leads to tangled problems of enforcement. The Environmental Defense Fund has recently spent hundreds of hours wading through the import documents attached to ivory shipments and has found that 80 percent are falsified or incorrectly filled out, for example, listing ivory from places like Hong Kong which have no elephants. Import documents are required to state the country of origin. EDF is preparing a lawsuit to force the government to keep better track of trade.

But it's a formidable task. US attorneys, more concerned about drug trafficking and organized crime, are reluctant to prosecute wildlife smuggling. Judges are hesitant to slap fines or prison sentences on offenders. The complexity of gathering evidence is overwhelming—a single fur-smuggling case a few years ago required attorneys to analyze 60,000 documents. And, Fish and Wildlife Service agents, the men responsible, are more accustomed to chasing duck hunters out of season than analyzing the business records of multinational import firms. The result is uneven enforcement. For example, Wayne King of the New York Zoological Society says that New York City, one of eight approved ports for wildlife trade, has strict controls. "But I could drive a herd of elephants through Los Angeles and the Fish and Wildlife Service director there wouldn't give a damn."

It sounds discouraging, but there is reason for modest hope. The Justice Department recently set up a task force with new authority to investigate illegal trade. The US World Wildlife Fund is raising money for a group called TRAFFIC USA to monitor the shipment of wildlife in and out of US ports. And 51 countries have now signed the Convention on International Trade in Endangered Species, a comprehensive treaty that lists endangered species, sets up rules for trading, shipping and monitoring traffic. Drawn up in 1973, the treaty has only recently begun to have an impact. Signatory nations agree to ban exports of wildlife in danger of extinction. Rare species may be traded under strict regulations. However, more than half the world's countries, including major wildlife traders such as Japan, Belgium, Italy and Mexico, haven't ratified the pact.

Solomon Ole Saibull, Tanzania's Minister for Natural Resources and Tourism, fears that "unless trade in endangered species is stopped, whole populations will disappear from the face of the earth."

The 1970s, Saibull said, "have brought despair to wildlife conservation throughout Central and Eastern Africa. The rising prices of ivory, rhino horns, leopard and zebra skins increased profits to unprecedented levels . . . The bulk of poached products is smuggled out of the country and sold on international markets beyond our control. A large amount of public revenue goes into unscrupulous private pockets."

In Africa, the trade has spawned a new breed of poacher armed with machine guns, light aircraft and friends in high places.

While Tanzania has a fairly good enforcement record, Kenya has experienced widespread official corruption. The Kenyatta family, which ruled the country for years, was alleged to be involved in the lucrative ivory trade. The World Bank reportedly held up a $17 million loan in an effort to oust John K. Mutinda, a high Kenyan wildlife official accused of protecting poachers. However, Mutinda remained in place and the loan, to beef up anti-poaching forces, was approved. Kenya recently closed souvenir shops which fostered illegal trade, but poaching for export continues.

The wildlife trade in South America has become a major political controversy. "One of the reasons some of our countries are bankrupt is due to the fact that our natural resources are extracted in such a way that we soon shall have nothing left," said Felipe Benavides, a Peruvian conservationist.

Peruvian officials recently confiscated 12 Humboldt penguins as they were being shipped from the airport for West Germany. Benavides believes as many as 300,000 pelts of guanacos, a llama-like animal, have been exported to West Germany.

"Every day we have Germans trying to buy their way to obtain caiman (alligator) skins through any means," Benavides said. "The bribery that goes on is shocking, but what is more shocking is that most of the bribers come from West Germany, Belgium and Holland."

Gabriel Seisdedos, a Chilean wildlife official, estimates that 15,000 fox, otter and other skins are illegally smuggled into Argentina every year. In Chile's remote Southern islands, he said, "the poachers threaten the inspectors with guns, so the inspectors run away."

At the most recent meeting of the Convention on International Trade in Endangered Flora and Fauna, held in Costa Rica in March, Surinam and Brazil sharply criticized West Germany and Great Britain for importing thousands of ocelot, margay and other cat skins smuggled out of the Amazon region.

"The developed countries which allow these illegal products have been notified of the illegality of this trade," protested the Surinam delegation in an official statement, "and yet these products continue to be imported."

West German officials and British customs said they are "looking into the matter."

Third world countries are not opposed to all animal killing, but when species are overexploited, they cease to be a commodity that can be harvested for continuous economic return. Brazil would eventually like to export crocodiles, but not when the species is threatened with extinction. In the case of Africa, tourism at the game parks, a major source of revenue, is adversely affected when there are no rhinos and zebras to be seen.

In the Far Eastern trading centers of Japan, Hong Kong and Singapore, wild animals are thought to have curative powers. In a Chinese medicine store, one can buy gall bladders of Malayan sun bears for liver problems, tiger bones to boil for a rheumatism potion, burned elephant skin to treat skin ulcers and deer antlers to enhance virility.

For many, animal smuggling raises issues beyond the conservation of species. "There's an immense amount of suffering," said Shirley McGreal, head of the International Primate Protection League in South Carolina. "To get baby monkeys you have to shoot the mother. The babies fall out of the trees and half the time they are killed."

Animals are tansported in tiny crates, frequently without enough food or water. They often arrive diseased and injured, according to Jean Yves Domalain, a former animal trader. He estimates that a third of the live animals traded die during their trips across continents and oceans to the zoos and pet stores of wealthy nations.

Spokesmen for the pet industry say the figures are exaggerated and that the animals are too valuable to be mistreated. The International Convention in Costa Rica, however, passed strict shipping standards to combat inhumane treatment.

While the animal trade has received the most international attention, a multimillion-dollar market for endangered plants is wiping out many species of flora around the world, biologists say.

Collectors will pay as much as $2,000 for a rare orchid. Arizona hires "cactus guards" to protect its desert saguaros. A West German tour company has sponsored collectors, trips to Mexico, during which entire hillsides are stripped bare of cacti.

Although the International Convention requires countries to monitor traffic in endangered plants, US trade is virtually unregulated because the Agriculture Department has denied funding for port inspectors. More than 400,000 pounds of ginseng, considered an aphrodisiac in Oriental countries, left the US in 1977. Only 4,000 pounds had legal permits, despite the fact the plant, which grows wild in Appalachia and is cultivated in the Midwest, has been severely depleted, according to the Natural Resources Defense Council.

It may be hard to work up a lather about ginseng. Or even about crocodiles. Elephants, rhinos, leopards, they have a certain romance about them—but cacti? That's the problem. We can get schoolchildren to write their congressmen to save the whales, but their mothers don't think twice about buying a Hawksbill tortoise shell hair comb. The road ahead seems to lead to more extinctions on the altar of consumerism.

CODDLING TROUT[3]

Sixty percent of the energy produced at the Public Service Electric and Gas Company's (PSE&G) coal-burning electrical generating station in Hamilton, New Jersey, was being wasted. It was going to heat the Delaware River.

To cool two massive steam turbine condensers, more than 450,000 gallons of water is sucked into the plant every minute; then discharged warmer by twelve degrees Fahrenheit. That wasted heat is a high price to pay for electrical energy, and a few scientists at the plant wondered how this situation could be remedied.

The solution was not simple, but the marketing studies indicated that if it succeeded, investment in a mariculture operation, using the warm effluent water from the 560 megawatt station, would soon make a profit.

[3] Article by Anthony S. Policastro, staff member of the *News Tribune*, New Jersey; freelance writer particularly on maritime subjects. *Oceans*. 12:27–8, Mr. '79. Copyright © 1970 by the Oceanic Society. All rights reserved. Reprinted with permission.

Research began on the massive project in 1973, on the theory that marine creatures not normally found in the northeast could be raised in the summer and fall, while growth of a cold-water species, such as rainbow trout could be accelerated in the winter and spring.

Conditions for the plan were ideal since the water temperature of the Delaware River varies seasonally from 32°F to 87°F. In addition, the water from the river is fresh despite the fact that it is a tidal body of water with a five- to six-foot tidal range—the salinity does not penetrate as far as the plant location. Chemical pollution is also of no concern since, with the exception of a small sewage treatment plant upriver, all of the polluters are downstream from the plant.

In July 1974, the National Science Foundation awarded PSE&G a $212,000 grant for aquaculture research, and the project was well on its way.

While aquaculture is not new in the United States (it first became popular in the 1960s), the kinds of marine creatures being raised today are novel. Trout and catfish farms have been flourishing in the United States for thirty years with Idaho producing most of the country's 30 million pounds of trout. Catfish farming is done primarily in Arkansas, Louisiana and Mississippi, with more than 1,000 catfish farmers raising eighty percent of the country's supply.

The new aquaculture focuses on the luxury seafoods—shrimp, lobster and oysters—rather than on species such as mullet, tilapia, and milkfish, which the American public finds unpalatable. The species chosen for the new aquaculture is dictated by its marketability; the sole motivation is a bottom line in the black.

PSE&G is not alone in trying to take advantage of otherwise wasted energy. More than 100 large corporations, including Union Carbide, Dow Chemical, Sun Oil, Seaboard utilities, Ralston Purina and Armour and Company, are experimenting with some type or other of aquaculture.

The initial research program showed that the PSE&G generating station could support giant subtropical shrimp (*Macrobrachium rosenbergii*) from May through October, and rainbow trout (*Salmo gairdneri*) during November through

April. Both of these marine animals are highly marketable, especially shrimp, in the United States. Americans consume more than one million pounds a day with sixty-five percent of that amount imported. Without control and replenishment the world's supply of shrimp could be completely devoured by Americans alone in a few years.

"The demand is insatiable," said Mark Evans, who manages PSE&G's aquaculture facility.

In November of 1976 a further sum from the National Science Foundation was used to construct a "proof-of-concept" facility. If it works, a commercially viable aquaculture facility should be operating by the early 1980s and capable of producing 144,000 pounds of trout (a density of 12 pounds of fish per cubic foot) during the six-month growing period. The plans call for the construction of fifty concrete fish raceways one hundred feet long, twelve feet wide and six feet deep. Research has been conducted jointly with PSE&G, Trenton State College, Rutgers University and the New Jersey Department of Agriculture. Long Island Oyster Farms provides shrimp larvae and feed for the project.

The present facility began with a crudely constructed thirty by ninety foot pond and a single concrete raceway sixty feet long. Two commercial sized raceways, one hundred feet long, were added later along with glass enclosed nurseries, a recirculation pond and a spider web of underground piping and pumps.

The intricate pumping system is capable of recirculating 3,100 gallons of discharge water through the raceways per minute, or mixing river water with the raceway water to drop the temperature in summer, when increased electrical loads raise the temperature of the station's outflow. The system also allows river water to be pumped directly into the raceways.

Water in the raceways is kept between 50°F and 68°F during the winter when the trout are grown, and between 75°F and 98°F in summer for the shrimp. The recirculation ponds retain warm discharge water for use in the raceways when the plant is shut down three times a day to chlorinate its steam turbine condensers.

Of the five aquatic animals experimented with at PSE&G,

the rainbow trout have been the most successful with an annual yield of 26,000 pounds of fish each weighing about 16 ounces. The fish grow about an inch every two months and increase about 4.4 ounces in weight. They survive at a density of three pounds per cubic foot.

All the species tested are fed animal protein in pellet form, except the eels which are given a mixture of fish meal and vitamins with plant gums as a binder, a feed that resembles mud.

Trout fingerlings and juveniles about seven inches long are supplied by the Musky Trout Hatchery in Bloomsbury, New Jersey, and introduced into the raceways in mid-November. They are not allowed to grow longer than ten inches; after that they begin to mature sexually and growth slows down considerably. The optimum water temperature is 68°F.

During the company's five-year testing programs, trout have proven to have the lowest mortality rate with very little bacterial diseases common to fish. They will become the main species cultured during the winter months after the plant constructs its full-scale facility in the 1980s.

"I expect we are about two or three years away from deciding if we want to go commercial with the trout," Evans said.

A new untested oxygen injection system will be constructed this winter with the hope that it will increase trout production threefold. They expect to harvest twelve pounds of fish per cubic foot when the new system is in operation. Testing has shown that low oxygen levels have been the limiting factor in trout growth. The oxygen system will supersaturate water from the raceways with liquid oxygen, and then reintroduce it into the ponds. The estimated cost of the additional oxygen is five cents per pound of fish.

Taste in raceway-grown trout is acceptable, but there is really nothing to compare it with since all New Jersey trout are hatchery grown and then introduced into natural ponds and waterways.

"I don't foresee taste as a marketing problem because it is not that different. Obviously, we can't duplicate what the fish eats when it's in a natural environment, but we can come close," Evans explained.

With the majority of the nation's trout being produced in the strong currents of Idaho's Snake River, PSE&G expects to have little trouble selling its projected harvests to markets on the east coast.

One of the less commercially successful species raised at the farm was the giant subtropical shrimp native to Southeast Asia. Initial testing proved so unprofitable, that the researchers were forced to discontinue large scale cultivation, and limit shrimp testing to indoor nursery tanks. The shrimp become cannibals when placed in high densities. If the animals are stocked any denser than one per square foot, mortality rates increase considerably. In addition, the growth cycle produces fifteen animals to the pound. The researchers also had problems finding a stable supply of live brine shrimp, the only diet of the shrimp during the larval stage.

Shrimp testing is conducted in two "greenhouses" where concrete burial vaults serve as habitats for the prawns. The group is also working on various plastic test compartments to be used to isolate the shrimp from each other.

Another problem with the prawns is getting them to molt, and hence grow, in captivity. Evans reported, "We had one that molted in a two by two by six-inch compartment, but that was only one out of a million."

The aquaculturists decided to replace the shrimp with the American catfish (*Ictalurus punctatus*) as its warm month species. In July 1978, 60,000 seven-inch fingerlings were placed in the two 100-foot raceways. The results were disastrous—only half survived. The fish were attacked by external parasites and contracted bacterial infections, probably because they were under stress from the higher densities.

"The thirty-six hour trip from Arkansas was no help either. So right from the start we were off on the wrong foot," Evans said. Although catfish is very popular in the southern part of the United States, Arkansas was the closest state that could supply 60,000 fingerlings.

The researchers were also hampered by the limited number of fish antibiotics they could use. Only two drugs are licensed and permitted by the federal Food and Drug Administration. Others exist, but they are not licensed and cannot be used since the fish are to be consumed by humans.

"The antibiotics we are allowed to use only eliminate the disease in the raceways, and don't cure the fish. So all those afflicted die off anyway. Part of the problem is that many drug manufacturers are not willing to invest in costly testing of new drugs unless there is a large market for them."

The next phase of research on the catfish involves hatching the eggs and raising the animals in high densities until they reach market size; about fourteen inches long and weighing about one pound.

"If they are born in crowded conditions, they will not be under stress if they stay in these conditions," Evans said. The research will be conducted this winter. They hope to harvest about eleven pounds of fish per cubic foot.

A peculiar species that the aquaculturists have had some success with is the American eel (*Anguilla rostrata*), which they began testing with the European and Japanese markets in mind. Of the first 800 or so eels weighing around one tenth of a pound, about the size of a pencil, sixty-two percent survived through every temperature range in the raceways. A year later the eels weighed approximately eight ounces.

The second batch of eels—18,000 smaller ones—were more susceptible to fungal infections and died, except for twenty which reached the size of a pencil. The animals were kept at a density approaching five per cubic yard. A third batch of the larger variety of juvenile eels was purchased in April 1978, and they are currently being raised in two glass-enclosed raceways. They expect that these eels will reach market size—about four-tenths of a pound—by June 1979.

The only problem with the eels is that the larger ones eat the smaller ones, but the scientists are currently working on graders which will segregate the elvers by size.

Only one species tested has been considered totally unacceptable. Striped bass (*Morone saxatilis*) have been abandoned. Of the first 4,000 seven to eight-inch fingerlings placed in the facility in December 1977 as a cold-month species, only twenty survived. The aquaculturists found that when the water temperature dipped below 40°F, the fish became extremely tense, ceased to feed and subsequently died from fungal infections. A second group of 6,000 bass fingerlings were tested again in June 1978 in the warmer raceway waters, but some 1,500 of these also succumbed to fungal disease.

The success of PSE&G's subsequent work in the new science will depend on whether it is feasible to raise marine creatures in a carefully-controlled environment, and whether resources invested will yield a sizeable profit. It appears that the aquaculturists at PSE&G are coming closer and closer to that goal.

TOWARD A BACKYARD FISH GARDEN[4]

Steve Van Gorder and fellow aquaculture researcher Jim Fritch had been up since dawn on that brisk morning last autumn. By nine o'clock both were feeling slightly chilled and damp, but nothing could dull the spirit of the moment. They worked deliberately, hauling in the heavy net and then counting the fish in the harvest. The task would take much longer than they had originally figured. They had to harvest 30 ponds in all—big blue swimming pools, really, the kind that families buy for their kids during the summer—and by the end of the day Van Gorder and Fritch would count almost 3,000 fish. Each catch was hauled to the side, where it was dumped into one of three holding tanks. At a nearby table, a man in a heavy slicker and sport fisherman's hat pulled a fish from the holding tank and weighed and measured it. An assistant wrote down the details on a notepad.

The man—Homer Buck, a well-known expert in Orien-

[4] Article by Anthony DeCrosta. *Organic Gardening and Farming.* 26:134–41. My. '79. Copyright 1979 by Rodale Press, Inc. All rights reserved. Reprinted with permission.

tal-style fish culture from Illinois—had designed the project, which took place at the Organic Gardening Research Center last summer. A few years ago, Dr. Buck showed that fish can be combined with animal husbandry to achieve excellent production. Adapting the methods of the Chinese, he fed Chinese carp nothing but algae created by fertilizing the pond water with pig manure. The manure, which washed directly into the ponds from pens on the bank, stimulated the growth of algae and plankton, natural food for the carp. In 1978, the aquatic biologist wanted to test this system again using chickens—much more practical on a small homestead—instead of swine. In addition, he tried a slightly different mix of fish species (called polyculture), various stocking densities, amounts of supplemental commercial feed and mechanical aeration.

Fish, like vegetables, need a healthy environment to thrive in. If you've ever owned an aquarium, you'll know what I mean. Take a fish, place it in a bowl of regular tap water and if it doesn't die within a few hours from the chlorine, it'll die in a few days from lack of oxygen. It's that simple. In a stream or mountain lake, fish are always supplied with fresh, oxygen-rich water, good food and a balance of fish companions. Different fish—like different crops in a companionate garden—not only can live together amicably, but also can benefit from each other. Various species feed on various levels of the aquatic food chain. Some fish, like the common carp, eat pond bottom organisms and the partially digested wastes of other fish, while others, like trout, need either commercial pellets or live foods such as insects and small crustaceans to survive. The algae (phytoplankton) and other minute plants in a natural lake help to keep the water clean by processing carbon dioxide and fish wastes into oxygen. Without these organisms, the fish would suffocate and poison themselves. A sublime balance is maintained. If there are too many fish for the water ecosystem to support, or if another element enters the system—the wastes from a chemical plant, for instance—the balance is disrupted and fish kills result. The same principle applies to fish cultivated in a confined area.

Dr. Buck and our aquaculturalists wanted to find the right combination of these variables that would lead to the highest production of fish in a small, closed system.

Pools Make Great Ponds

Because building 30 absolutely identical small ponds to meet scientific standards was impractical, the researchers conducted their investigation in conventional, vinyl-lined swimming pools. Each measured 12 feet across and three feet deep. After these "ponds" were erected on a gravel-based area unshielded from sun or wind, the bottoms were covered with about an inch of screened clay-loam topsoil, which serves as a breeding ground for digestible worms or insect larvae. Each pool was filled with 1,600 gallons of well water.

At this stage of the experiment, all the pools were exactly alike. The only differences in the study would be those aspects of fish culture the researchers wished to investigate. Ten trials would be run—matching different environmental factors with both monocultures and polycultures. Having 30 pools was a way to triple-check the results of each trial.

The researchers weren't able to raise the mix they wanted to use most. "The best polyculture that anybody knows about are the three types of Chinese carp," Van Gorder told me. "The grass carp, silver carp and big-head carp feed on different biological levels, and they utilize more natural foods than other fish we know of." But the Chinese carp are outlawed in many states, including Pennsylvania (one exception is Arkansas, which uses the exotic fish for biological weed control). Trout—another fish popular with many breeders—likes cold water, and is not well adapted in still-water cultivation. "Picking the proper fish for the temperature range is the key to outdoor fish raising," Fritch explained.

Our study involved combinations and stocking densities of Israeli carp (a fast-growing variety of common carp) or channel catfish and special all-male tilapia. Each species feeds on different levels of the food chain. For instance, the carp consumes anything it can scrounge off the bottom, in-

cluding raw manure and the fecal material from other fish.
Some species of tilapia, a tropical variety of fish, like to eat
grass clippings, algae or garden wastes, and so are cheaper to
produce than some meat-eaters like trout. The tilapia's main
drawback is that it will die if the water temperature drops
below 50 degrees F. A monosex hybrid type was used to avoid
reproduction and maintain stable densities. As an alternative
to that system, a more conventional polyculture with channel
catfish (which eat commercial feed) was grown. Both catfish
and carp are available from hatcheries and fish nurseries. Tilapia brood stock can be purchased at many aquarium supply
stores and pet shops.

Eight of each series of ten test pools were fertilized by
chicken manure. "Fertilizing has always been the best way to
create a balanced ecosystem," Van Gorder explained. "The
chickens that we used were raised in cages—two to a cage,
which provided them with much more room than they normally have in a battery cage." The coops were set directly
over the pools that were to receive fertilization. Fish in fertilized ponds also got supplemental feed at a rate of 2 percent
of their body weight. Fish in unfertilized ponds got 5 percent.
In one trial, a monoculture of tilapia grew in fertilized water
but got no supplemental feed.

Although keeping fish stock well nourished is essential,
supplying them with oxygen can't be ignored. They can actually live much longer without food than they can without
oxygen. Fisheries biologist Andy Merkowsky of Rodale Resources—which designed compact mechanical aerators for
the project—agrees. "The biggest problem the fish farmer
faces today is oxygen," he told me. "Most fish farmers produce about 2,000 pounds of fish per acre. Certain farmers get
as much as 3,000 pounds, but they're finding that the water
table is dropping as they pump more and more fresh water
into their ponds. One man I know is getting 9,000 pounds per
acre from his 25-acre pond, and sometimes as much as 15,000
pounds per acre. He uses aeration."

Just why aeration is necessary for a smaller system is not
difficult to understand. Algae and naturally-occurring green

plants in a pond produce oxygen during the day. At night, when photosynthesis stops, no oxygen is produced and the supply gradually runs down. But the fish and other pond life still need oxygen to live. In an intensive fish cropping system, fish wastes unused by plankton and the vigorous bloom of algae itself can block the sunlight during the day, and kill off the algae at lower levels. As that algae dies, the amount of ammonia (from the wastes) rises and the amount of oxygen declines as bacteria work on dead algae. It is a critical time. Fish can die.

"Another trouble time for fish farmers is in late July and early August," Merkowsky continued. "The air is hot, and hot water holds less oxygen than cold water. The fish are getting bigger and more active at this time of the year and demand more oxygen."

Seven of each series of ponds in our test project were provided with very small mechanical aerators, a 1/20 horsepower unit. The units were used only at nights. "The aerators were not run 24 hours a day—that comes to less than a dime a day—I think this is significant," remarked Fritch.

Polycultures Raise Yields

What we found out from last year's small-scale aquaculture project follows the organic gardener's rule-of-thumb —the more diversified the system, the higher the yields. Polycultures worked better than monocultures, as a trial combining carp with tilapia compared to carp raised alone proved. The feces of the tilapia, which fed on algae, contained much semidigested plankton, which provided a bonus to the bottom-feeding carp. Individual carp weights were higher when grown this way, although tilapia did better with catfish than with carp.

Mechanical aeration was also shown to be a tremendous advantage. Fish supplied with extra oxygen—whether in monoculture or polyculture—grew faster and were healthier than those raised in nonaerated ponds. "We had anaerobic conditions in pools without aerators," said Van Gorder.

"Nightly use of aerators eliminated oxygen gradients, and the fish ate better and were under less stress."

The beneficial influence of chicken manure was most apparent in test trials involving carp and tilapia. Both pools were aerated. Both received supplemental feed. Despite higher rations in the trial *not* using fertilization, the carp and tilapia raised with chickens were significantly larger and had a higher survival rate. Fertilization also cut down food costs by one-third to one-half. One side benefit of using chickens to fertilize the ponds was especially economical—1,820 eggs were produced (by 48 pullets) during the 77-day experiment.

Supplemental feed was beneficial in pools enriched by manure only if the pools were aerated. If they were not aerated, ammonia levels went up in the water and oxygen levels fell.

Which trial pond fared the best? Without doubt, the biggest gains in numbers and individual weights of fish occurred in the pool that combined Israeli carp with tilapia. This pool was aerated and was fertilized by chickens. A 2 percent commercial food supplement was given.

The production in that pond was only 13 pounds of live fish. Dick Harwood, director of the Organic Gardening Research Center, explained that there were two reasons for this year's low yields. "The fingerlings that were stocked were too small for optimum growth. They were each two to three inches long. The stock should have been at least four inches each, as their potential for growth is much higher at that stage," he said. "Another reason for the low figures was the shortness of our growing season. Because of a late start, the project had only a 77-day duration. If we had had a full growing season, we would have gotten much higher yields."

"Our study indicates that eventually a backyard fish gardener with a small pool can raise 50 to 100 pounds of fish in half a year," Steve Van Gorder told me recently. By refining the system they developed last year, our researchers are confident that they will be able to do just that. "We really don't know the ultimate productive capacity of the system," he added.

We'll be running two projects this summer. The outdoor

one—using 40 pools at the New Farm and eight in the backyards of local residents—will test for the best polyculture stocking densities and the effectiveness of greenhouse dome-like enclosures to increase the length of the growing season and the maximum water temperature. Because last year we found high productivity by mixing different fish species, several alternate types of fish will also be cultivated. A new, more efficient aerator prototype will be used. "We're testing many methods of aquaculture because we're trying to discover the most economically and technologically sound system for fish gardeners," Van Gorder said.

Another fish project—possibly even more productive, eventually—has been taking place indoors. There is one major difference (and added cost) between indoor and outdoor aquaculture: Because algae will not normally grow indoors, a special recirculating-filtration system must be used to remove the buildup of poisonous fish wastes in the water. Although it's not as simple as growing fish outside, indoor fish raising is really not as difficult as it sounds. "It's like a big aquarium," Jim Fritch explained. "But instead of an aquarium filled with pretty exotic fish, people can raise species that they eat." Two 9-by-7-foot tanks in a basement corner at Rodale Resources produced almost 100 pounds of fish in five months last year.

We're continuing to work on a simple, home fish-gardening kit. When we feel the system proves able to provide a family with several hundred pounds of backyard fish, the kit will be made available.

Can fish gardening work for you? "A lot of people set up swimming pools or goldfish ponds in their backyards," Jim Fritch said. "What we're trying to do is get them to turn those things into something productive."

A pond is rich with colors and can make a harmonious addition to a garden. Fish and vegetables complement each other in another, more basic way. Vegetable scraps can serve as food for certain types of fish, while the nutrient-rich waste water from a fish pond can benefit garden soil. "It will surely increase the average garden's productivity," says Dick Harwood. . . .

BLOODY HARVEST[5]

Each year, around the first week in March, female harp seals of the North Atlantic haul themselves out of frigid waters off the east coast of Canada to whelp. Each bears a single pup. A week or two later the men come. In what will appear a brutal and inhumane scenario to newcomers—and to many veteran observers as well—hunters will pummel the heads of the newborn seals. Within two weeks, more than half the pups will be dead—the harvest of licensed hunters.

Like whaling, the harp-seal hunt was once unrestricted. But the decline of the herd in the late 1950s—from an estimated 3,300,000 to 1,250,000—ultimately led to quotas on the number of animals that could be killed. The herd, which now numbers close to 1.4 million seals (excluding the newborn), is managed by Canada and the European Economic Community (the range of the herd extends north to Greenland, which is governed by Denmark, an EEC member). This year the quota is set at 180,000 animals: 150,000 for Canadians, 20,000 for Norwegians, and 10,000 for native Eskimos of Canada and Greenland. (Subsistence hunting by Eskimos is not restricted, but the average annual Eskimo take is factored in when setting the quota.) Nearly 80 percent of the kill will involve pups, most younger than 21 days old. Pups are prized for their downy-soft, snow-white fur, which they will begin to shed when three weeks old.

Citing the harp-seal hunt as an economic and nutritional necessity to his constituents, Brian Peckford, Newfoundland's Minister of Mines and Energy, toured the United States and Europe earlier this year defending the controversial "harvest" of Canada's seal "fishery." Accompanied by biologist Mac Mercer, senior Canadian policy advisor on sealing, he met with journalists to "set the record straight" on what his

[5] Article by Janet Raloff, policy/technology editor. Science News. 115:202-4. Mr. 31, '79.

government claims are emotional and inaccurate charges being leveled against Canada and its sealers.

Not surprisingly, environmentalists have responded with an intense counter campaign. To them Canada is promoting wanton exploitation of defenseless animals. And for what, they ask, is this species being pushed to extinction? To become the lining of a New Yorker's glove, the fob on a European's key chain, or perchance the extravagant robe for a pampered Westerner's body.

Charges fly back and forth between the opposing sides. But the fever pitch witnessed in the past few weeks has no doubt been heightened by a campaign the Fund For Animals started last November. Its mass mailing to millions of persons in the United States and elsewhere calls for a boycott of tourism to Canada until the sealing stops.

It's easy to understand the emotional aspects of this issue. Sealing is a multi-million dollar industry for Newfoundland and Labrador and a tradition for "landsmen" in their coastal communities. On the other side, few animals are so photogenic as the white-coated, dewey-eyed harp seal; few scenes so gruesome as watching men bash in the heads of cute baby animals. But what will confuse anyone trying to sort through the issues objectively is the barrage of statistics and scientific findings that each side offers. This "evidence" is at best highly contradictory.

A good example is the debate over the harp seal's future. While no group claims the herd is in danger of immediate extinction, many animal-welfare groups charge that the North Atlantic harp seal stock has already been decimated and that unless a moratorium on killing is enacted soon, the population may not be large enough to sustain itself against the competing threats of pollution, disease and predation

Meanwhile, the Canadian government contends that the harp-seal quota is below the maximum sustainable yield (MSY)—or the number that could be killed each year and still permit the population to maintain its current size. As such, Canada claims the stock will slowly increase in size. The goal is 1.6 million seals, Mercer told *Science News*, and "at current scientific projections, we could expect that to occur in five to ten years."

Who is right? David M. Lavigne, a zoologist at the University of Guelph in Ontario, is an expert on harp seals. His work and opinions are quoted frequently by environmentalists and Canadian-hunt defenders alike. He says most analyses suggest the herd declined "substantially" between 1950 and 1970. "The Canadian government maintains that the herd has been increasing in number since 1972. That's one interpretation, but I don't believe we have enough information to know what the herd's been doing. The problem is that the analyses that suggest the population is increasing come from mathematical assessments and computer models." But what happens to harp seals in a computer may not be what happens to harp seals in the North Atlantic, he says.

There should be measurable changes in a herd that is either increasing or decreasing in size, he says, such as changes in growth rates, rates of maturation and whelping success—"those sorts of things that we refer to as being density dependent. In other words, if there are fewer animals in the population, then young animals grow at a fast rate and mature earlier than if there are a lot of animals competing with each other."

"Because harp seals take five to seven years to reach maturity, there are time lags before you can actually measure the effects of change in population size," he says. "I would add, though, even if we did see changes in such things as age at maturation or change in growth rates, these could be attributed to other than population changes. For example, the carrying capacity of the northwest Atlantic may not be as high as it was."

Lavigne has been critical of his government's sealing policy. The government says the herd must increase because its quota is below the MSY, he says, "but I question whether there is such a thing [as an MSY] for the harp seal." He suspects the current sealing quota is too high and causing a decline in the herd. "The one thing you have to remember about the harp seal is that it's a vastly depleted stock."

Lavigne also worries about what the effects of taking more and more fish from the sea may be doing not only to the seals, but also to the fish stocks. "The situation of many fish stocks off the east coast of Canada is worse than that of the harp seal," he says, citing the capelin as an example. Canadian capelin catches increased during the 1970s "from in excess of about 6,000 metric tons to in excess of 360,000 metric tons over a couple of years. Then last year it dropped . . . and this year they had to close the fishery," he said.

The Canadian government worries about the same problem but sees it differently. Explaining that the diet of the harp seal and that of humans have much in common, the Canadian government has claimed—and some Canadian fishermen claim this also—that seals are depleting Canadian fishing stocks. Mac Mercer says his government estimates that harp seals eat about two million tons of fish per year. "That's more food—fish and other marine life—than the total catch of all the nations fishing in the area. So it's a very signficant part of the system."

Nonsense, says Lavigne. "The problem is not seals, it's man and his fishing. We need to feed people, but at some point in time, *Homo sapiens* is going to have to realize that he has to limit his numbers or Mother Nature will do it for him."

But the two biggest issues over which the Canadian government and environmentalists differ have nothing to do with seal diets or biology. They are whether the hunt is necessary and whether it's humane.

At his January press conference, Peckford said Newfoundland fishermen live in a region with "no industry, no commerce, no agriculture, no mining, and no forestry to turn to when winter closes in." And the six weeks of sealing is the fisherman's only opportunity "to add to an income pitifully small at best," he said. What's more, "the harp seal provides a source of fresh meat for many . . . during a time of year when it is difficult to obtain other fresh meat."

But looking only at the issue of income, many ask if the government wouldn't fare better financially if it were to subsidize fishermen for not taking seals—as many Canadian and

US farmers are now paid not to plant certain crops. Income from the hunt to sealers for pelts, meat and oil came to only $3.4 million last year, Mercer says. Cleveland Amory of the Fund For Animals charges that most of that money didn't go to landsmen, but to the big factory ships who then doled out meager wages to their workers. And Lavigne parrots others in his concern that defending the seal hunt costs the government more than the hunt itself nets.

"When you start adding up the cost of flying government-sponsored public-relations firms around the world to tell people how good it is to hunt harp seals, that's got to cost hundreds of thousands of dollars. When you accompany sealing vessels with ice breakers to get them into the herds and fly scientists back and forth to assess the populations, that costs money." Add to that the cost of information booklets produced by the government at between $30,000 and $50,000 and mailed to people asking about the hunt, or the cost of enforcement officers at the hunt site. "If you're going to evaluate the true value of an industry you have to add up the inputs as well as the outputs, and with the present market value for seal pelts (in fact, they've been stockpiling pelts), I just don't think they're making any money doing it," Lavigne says.

Peckford had also said that no part of the seal is wasted. Its meat is eaten and its blubber used for oil. "Absolute garbage," Lavigne says. "The bulk of the carcasses are left on the ice, although there's a growing tendency to use more." He says Canadians are being encouraged to try seal-flipper TV dinners, but that seal meat isn't eaten in the quantities the government would have one believe. And an editorial in Newfoundland's largest newspaper, the Evening Telegram, bears this out. "If it becomes generally known that seal meat is not being used for food, we will be knocking away one of the props in our case for the seal fishery."

The cruelty issue is more complicated. Clubbing seals is "bloody, yes,—inhumane, no!" according to Peckford. He said, "It was found after extensive research that the most humane way to kill seals is by using the club, quickly followed by bleeding out. And that is exactly how your own government kills thousand of Alaskan seals every year: by the club."

"Your own Department of Agriculture, the American Academy of Sciences [sic], the Humane Society of the United States, the Bureau of Sports Fisheries and Wildlife [sic] and the Bureau of Commercial Fisheries conducted the tests," he continued. "These tests included numerous methods: electrocution, captive bolt, gunshot and carbon-dioxide asphyxia. These findings have all been substantiated again by six veterinarians who served on a panel of the American Veterinary Medical Association. You name it, the method has been tried, and all experts agree the club is still the most humane method."

That's true in theory, but not in practice, says Patricia Forkan, vice president of the Humane Society of the United States. Brian Davies, head of the International Fund For Animal Welfare, agrees and explains why: "First you have animals, maybe five days old; there are two kinds of behavior these young seals are apt to adopt. One is the 'play dead' stance, much like a possum." Here pups essentially stop breathing and draw their heads back into the fat surrounding their shoulders. "At this point there is a very thick layer of blubber covering their heads. It's difficult to kill a seal when it does that. The other behavior, and it seems to occur about 50 percent of the time, is to aggressively snap at the hunter. Then you've got a moving target, difficult to hit."

It's essential that the skull be crushed to ensure instant brain death and so the animals won't feel pain when skinning occurs immediately afterward.

"The Canadian Government never tells you that a good many thousand seals—you can never get the exact figure—are caught in nets and drowned," Davies adds. "No mention's ever made of that because even the Canadian government wouldn't suggest that it's humane."

Davies has observed the Canadian hunt each year for the past twelve. "Men that I've talked to say that for every seal that they hit and recover, they lose five that escape beneath the ice—big animals," Davies recounts. He fears many may die or be seriously hurt. In any case, he says, those clubbed and not killed have clearly experienced inhumane treatment at the hands of the clubbers.

Sue Pressman, director of wildlife protection for the Humane Society of the United States, worries that some harp seal pups might be skinned alive, after viewing the Canadian hunt. Unlike the US fur-seal hunt in Alaska (involving 30,000 animals a year), the harp seal is killed and skinned instantly, before there is time to check whether the animal is even unconcious. And one man does it all, she complains. In contrast, teams of men work on the kill in Alaska. If one man tires, another starts clubbing so that a firm and potentially lethal blow is delivered each time. And, because the animal is bled for an hour prior to skinning, there can be little doubt about whether it is dead.

The British Royal Society for the Prevention of Cruelty to Animals is also concerned. It sent its wildlife advisory officer, veterinary pathologist Bill Jordan, to observe the 1978 Canadian hunt. On the first day that he examined skulls of recently killed pups, he found 7 of 13 had not been fractured even though several had received repeated blows to the head and ears. One animal showed a corneal reflex causing Jordan to ask in his report, "Was it therefore conscious when its throat was cut and it was skinned?" In his report, Jordan remarks that after the first day all skulls he looked at had been crushed, although "many had been crushed after death . . . by the heel of a boot."

While the claims of sealers and protesters volley back and forth, another issue is quietly exerting growing pressure on the Canadian government. Already 250,000 postcards responding to the Fund For Animals' boycott Canada campaign have been received by Canada's Prime Minister Pierre Trudeau. While total proceeds of last year's harp-seal hunt totaled $5.5 million, US tourists spent $1.5 *billion* in Canada last year. "The [boycott] campaign poses a major threat to Canada's efforts to cut back the mammoth $625 million deficit it suffered in tourist trade with the United States last year," according to the November 29, 1978, Toronto *Star*.

A March 2, 1979, follow up in the same paper put it more succinctly: "The deciding factor in the future of the seal hunt may be neither animal suffering, the fisheries' survival, nor the extinction of the species but national economics. . . . Whether the boycott and [European ban on imported pelts] succeed may ultimately depend on the emotional response of foreign TV viewers to the sight of baby seal blood splattering on snow-covered ice."

V. RECREATION: PET OR PREY, PLEASURE OR PAIN?

EDITOR'S INTRODUCTION

Since animals are now widely accepted as helpmates, companions, and psychological allies, the hunting of animals, long a popular form of recreation, is under increasing challenge by those who regard the sport as immoral.

The first two articles in this section were contributed by Nelson Bryant, outdoors editor of the New York *Times*. In the first article, from *Atlantic Monthly*, Bryant analyzes the urges that motivate people to hunt, and he concludes that the sport is basically "a manifestation of man's drive to reestablish or maintain a union with the natural world." In the second article from the *Times*, he documents the extremes of emotion that the subject of hunting invariably arouses in the public and then he attempts to show how this activity can be justified in a modern society.

The third selection, titled "100 Million Dogs and Cats" in *U.S. News and World Report*, provides a set of alarming statistics about an "innocent phenomenon gone out of control."

The next two articles discuss the therapeutic effect of pets on people. Lawrence Galton, writing in *Parade*, found that the revolutionary practice of pet-facilitated therapy for humans, in which pets and patients are paired off, has actually improved the health and outlook of the seriously ill and aged. In the second article, from *American Education*, Judith Rosenfeld reveals how responses in physically and mentally handicapped children were greatly improved in an innovative program of horseback riding.

BEHOLD THE HUNTER[1]

Outside the log cabin, dawn arrives reluctantly. The light snow that fell the day before has nearly disappeared in the overnight thaw, and a cold, gray mist shrouds the upper portions of the mountains that surround us.

One by one, my four deer-hunting companions depart. I am left alone and the only sound breaking the silence of our wilderness hideaway is the snapping of burning chunks of hardwood in the heavy cast-iron stove that once served the cook in a logging camp. Lighted anew each morning when we rise at 4:30, it soon makes the place so warm I am forced to remove my woolen shirt in order to be comfortable.

The stove's efficiency delights me—one needs to stoke it only about every two hours—and over the years I have baked bread, pies, and biscuits in its capacious oven and have had many good soups and chowders simmering on its back corners. The odor of woodsmoke creeping from it, a sweet-sad aroma that evokes memories of good friends and good times in years past, also touches, I like to believe, something lurking in my genes from the time when my hunting forebears squatted on their haunches about an open fire.

In this place, the far reaches of northern New Hampshire, we hunt deer in the classic manner, each man moving through the woods alone, matching his stamina and powers of observation against those of the animal pursued. (I use the word "classic" in a limited sense, for it applies only to that period which began a few hundred years ago, when gunpowder and the musket or rifle enabled one man to hunt alone with a relatively high degree of success. In the beginning when fruit- and nut-eating man lost his forest habitat because of encroaching ice and cold weather and was forced to hunt on the open grasslands—there was no way he could suc-

[1] Article by Nelson Bryant, columnist, the New York *Times*. *Atlantic Monthly*. 240:66–70. D. '77. Copyright © 1977, by The Atlantic Monthly Company, Boston, Mass. Reprinted with permission.

ceed except by joining others in an effort not unlike today's deer drive.) Here we do not indulge in the deer drives so common in the low country, where patches of wood surrounded by meadows or farmland lend themselves to such endeavors; where gangs of men move noisily—or at least with no attempt at stealth—through likely deer habitat, pushing the animals toward others waiting on stand. Even if we wished to stage a drive, we would need a regiment to do so in the wild country we hunt, for hardwoods and conifers stretch in unbroken ranks for mile upon mile through river valleys and across mountains dark in the distance.

Reluctant to tackle my notebook, I have wasted as much time as I can justify in feeding the fire and adjusting the damper, but am given a short reprieve when a snowshoe rabbit appears from under the hemlocks at a corner of the clearing outside. He has a rather disreputable appearance—like one who has clothed himelf at a rummage sale—for this is the time of year when his brown pelt of summer begins to turn white. This shift, triggered by the shortening hours of daylight, will continue until he is almot pure white except for the tips of his ears. For a moment—thinking of a rabbit pie—I contemplate shooting him, but one varying hare would only be enough for two men.

Two hours later, my writing done, I pick up my muzzle-loading rifle and powder horn and leave for the mountain ridge east of camp. There are sometimes as many deer near the bottom of the ridge, but getting to the summit is a climb I enjoy.

I will never become a truly expert deer hunter—and I have been at it for thirty-five years—because I cannot shuck off the thoughts and images of the civilized world in which most of my life is spent, cannot become a total predator naked of any emotion save the desire to kill.

That day, the last mist-draped rocky height achieved, I was more preoccupied than usual and the urge to hunt was muted. I laid the rifle and the powder horn on a fallen, moss-covered log beside me and wondered why I had chosen to go forth with them rather than with the modern high-powered rifle complete with telescopic sight that I had also brought to the cabin. Was I merely engaging in a silly game that had no real meaning? Was the choice of the antique weapon, which certainly limited my chance of success, an indication that I did not really want to kill, or was I trying to make the hunt more real by using a rifle from an era when the hunter's role was important to his family's survival?

Was I a pathetic middle-aged man attempting to obscure with ritual an act that no longer had any validity?

The answer to these questions—after long deliberation during which I shared a bag of peanuts with a friendly chipmunk, and after many more contemplative hours in the next four days—was no, and following is some of the terrain I covered in my quest for self-understanding.

I cannot, to begin with, forget the controversial television film of 1975, *The Guns of Autumn*. After a private screening of the film prior to its public release, I returned to my desk and wrote in the first two paragraphs of my Wood, Field and Stream column for the New York *Times:*

If one were planning to portray the glories of love between man and woman in a television documentary, then devoted the entire show to the antics of a drunken clod in a bordello, one would achieve the same level of truth realized in the CBS News 90-minute film, The Guns of Autumn.

Purporting to be a fair example of hunting in America, the show instead focused on the shooting of bears in a city dump, the hurly-burly of opening day at a public waterfowl hunting area, running a bear with hounds, Jeeps and two-way radios, then keeping the animal treed until the women and children can gather about to witness the kill, and the slaughter of exotic big game animals in a mile-square preserve on the outskirts of Detroit.

The show troubled me deeply because I had to believe that those who made it truly felt that they were offering an honest portrayal of hunting in the United States, and if they, as trained newsmen, could be so misled, what of the attitudes held by the public toward hunting?

I knew, of course, that of the estimated 20 million hunters in this country there are certainly a signficant number whose hunting and shooting skills are virtually nonexistent, whose manner is boorish, and whose knowledge of the creatures they seek to kill, and of the natural world, is minimal.

I contrast the so-called hunting slobs with my aforementioned four hunting friends moving silently through the mountains and valleys observing everything, for they are excellent woodsmen. When they return to the cabin at dark, they will, whether successful or not, warm slowly to their stories of what they have seen and done. One evening one of them arrived an hour after sundown and it was not until he was halfway through his supper that we learned the reason for his tardiness: he had lost time dragging a deer three miles down the mountain to the bank of a river a mile from camp, from which spot the animal was retrieved the next day with the aid of a cartop boat.

Much of the anti-hunting sentiment in this country is directed against the deer hunter, probably because he and his slain quarry are highly visible. Also, deer are lovely, graceful creatures with whom everyone can empathize.

The annual whitetail and mule deer (the latter in the Midwest, West, and Far West) kill by hunters in recent years has averaged about 2,225,000 animals. In the East, Pennsylvania and New York are the leading whitetail states, with a respective average kill of about 140,000 and 100,000 animals each year. In New York, some 650,000 deer hunters went forth last year, including archers and those with muzzle-loading and modern firearms.

Although a few hunters may gain some gratification from displaying the evidence of their success, most, I believe, would rather get the deer home, butchered, and into the freezer with a minimum of public attention. But in many states the law requires that all or a portion of a deer be displayed during transportation. In the Northeast, only three states, Pennsylvania, Rhode Island, and Vermont, allow hunters to conceal all of a deer during transportation. New York goes from one extreme to the other in this wise. Any deer taken on a regular license in New York may be completely out of sight while being moved. This kill usually accounts for about 55 percent of the total. The remaining 45 percent are those shot under the so-called deer management permits, and those animals must be carried completely outside the car or in the open bed of a pickup truck. In Connecticut, the law requiring slain deer to be visible does not apply to those taken under crop-protection permits. The basic argument for having deer visible during transportation is that it gives law enforcement officers a legitimate reason for stopping a car to check licenses and firearms. Such a law clearly exists for the protection of deer, but some fish and game officials—usually those not involved with law enforcement—feel that eliminating the anti-hunting sentiment generated by the parade of dead animals is more important than gaining assistance in apprehending lawbreakers.

Richard Cronin of the Massachusetts Division of Fisheries and Wildlife tells of the woman who called him to say that while she had never been opposed to hunting, she had to report that driving along the highway behind a car bearing a dead deer had literally made her ill, given her nightmares that evening, and deeply disturbed the children riding with her.

I recall returning from a deer-hunting trip in New Hampshire with my brother a few years ago. That state's law says that only a portion of the creature must be visible, so we put our deer in the back of my suburban wagon with only one hoof showing out the back window. That was enough, however, to cause a pretty girl driving a sports car to pull alongside us, sound her horn, and then salute us with the one-fingered international gesture of disdain.

Deer hunters themselves are often very visible, and when they reach high concentrations they can be disturbing to the eye and the sensibilities. During deer week on the island of Martha's Vineyard, where I live the woods are filled with yelping, howling men driving deer. Shotguns boom throughout the day and the slugs from them snap and whine through the scrub oaks and pitch pines. Nearly every roadside has its platoons of unkempt men, each wearing a fluorescent orange vest and usually a hat of the same color. This clownlike garb, which adds a strident note to the whole enterprise, is distaste-

ful to many hunters, myself among them, but it is required by
law in a number of states, including Massachusetts, and even
where it is not mandatory hunters often wear it for self-pro-
tection. Fluorescent orange, which shows up at incredible
distances in the woods even in bad light, has proved effective
in preventing hunters from shooting each other.

Until quite recently, I thought that most of the resistance
to hunting came from those who believed that certain species
were being endangered or those who could not stomach the
idea that anyone could gain pleasure from a pursuit in which
the ultimate goal is the killing of some bird or animal.

But a recent survey by Batten, Barton, Durstine and Os-
born, Inc. of New York City for the National Shooting Sports
Foundation seems to reveal that the average non-hunter is
not opposed to the killing of wild game per se, but feels 1)
that too many hunters are so inept that they wound birds or
animals which later die an agonizing death; 2) that because
many hunters are untrained they are dangerous to protected
species, including men; and 3) that many hunters discard the
trappings of civilization when afield, trespassing, destroying
property, and, in general, behaving like boors.

Most informed observers of the hunting scene in the
United States would probably agree that almost without exception no species of bird or animal threatened with extinction is being hunted. Game management techniques and the
laws that implement them have the situation in hand.

Near the end of the last century in New York State, for
example, the whitetail deer herd in the Catskills was nonexistent, and the same was nearly true of the Adirondack herd.
The unprotected animals had been pushed out or eliminated
by early farmers who not only cleared land and destroyed
deer habitat but also relied heavily on the animals for meat.
In the Adirondacks, logging camp operators used the whitetail as a major source of food. In 1912, a New York State law
making it illegal to shoot does was passed, and, with certain
exceptions (including the aforementioned management permits), has been in effect ever since.

Clearly, the recent average annual kill of about 100,000

deer in New York indicates the validity of management techniques and demonstrates also that the species is not endangered.

Why not, some argue, simply stop hunting deer? This could be done. The herds throughout the nation would double almost overnight, and then, having exceeded the capacity of the range to sustain them, millions of animals would die of starvation. Eventually, deer populations would dwindle to what the damaged habitat could sustain. The deer would also, for many years, be smaller and less healthy than they are at the present time.

Some dedicated anti-hunters suggest that we simply have professional hunters to kill the excess deer and turn the meat over to needy people. But the hunter feels that members of his fraternity have contributed—through, among other things, license fees, taxes on sporting arms and ammunition, membership in conservation groups, purchase of federal duck stamps, and gifts to Ducks Unlimited—more than any other single group to the cause of the creatures he pursues. He also feels that he probably has a better understanding of the natural world and a greater love for it than does the average non-hunter. Therefore he reacts in various ways to the attack launched against him by such groups as the Fund for Animals and the Friends of Animals. Some lash out angrily, some retreat into silence, others attempt a reasoned explanation of their sport.

Most American hunters come from rural backgrounds wherein going afield with gun and dog was as natural to them as haunting the neighborhood pool hall was to their urban counterparts. But even the man who is steeped in the tradition of hunting sometimes, particularly as he grows older, becomes less interested in a full game bag than in the mystique of the hunt. It may be that when the first flush of young manhood is over, when the body begins its inevitable decline, one gains a new sense of the fragility of life. Or it may also happen that some personal experience, perhaps shooting an animal that escapes to die a lingering death, makes a man curtail or end his hunting.

During World War II, while recuperating in a hospital in Wales after taking a machine gun bullet through the chest a few days after my parachute infantry regiment dropped into Normandy, I resolved that I would never again pull the trigger on a living thing, man or beast. But between that June and that September body and spirit partially mended. I left the hospital just in time to make the jump into Holland, and when I went home after the war I returned to hunting.

I would be dissembling if I said that shooting a bird or an animal brings me pure pleasure, and many hunters experience a twinge of uneasiness at the sight of a dying or dead animal. With the hoped-for culmination comes a feeling of regret, sometimes even a vague fear that something is wrong. But all meat-eating men, hunters or not, are caught in this enigma, and it seems absurd to suggest that the man who buys his meat or fowl at the market and thereby avoids the ultimate encounter—the death of the creature he consumes—is a more honorable or sensitive fellow than one who slaughters his own pigs or shoots his own game.

I have even felt squeamish when the cold, taut body of a lovely trout shudders in my hand after I rap its head with a stick. But this never-ending cycle of birth and dying, of one specie providing food for another, is inescapable. To live, I must consume something that was once alive, and to live fully, I must, at present, continue to hunt.

I eat everything I kill, or, if I am far from home and cannot get the game back, give it to someone who will. For most of us, however, hunting for food is not a reasonable justification for the pursuit. We would do much better, from an economic point of view, to go to the corner market.

What is a man who in one week can be entranced by a Beethoven symphony, a Manet, a line of poetry, and in the next be equally caught up in following the trail of a wild animal through the snow-filled woods? The mind reels at trying to embrace this. Vague images form, re-form, and dissolve, and what finally comes to us, if we are fortunate, is a creature wisdom that allows us to live with what we can only dimly comprehend.

In some of us the primal urge for the chase survives, and it is not the result of a disordered psyche or repressed sexuality. (A woman wrote me after one of my hunting columns appeared: "Good luck, big boy! You're another of those little men running through the woods with the only gun in your hand that will ever go off!")

As I look back on my deer-hunting of last season, it seems clear that I was not consumed by lust of any description. I carried my muzzle-loading rifle with me through eight days of hunting in southwestern New Hampshire and another five days in the northern part of the state, and during that time I had only one glimpse of an animal, at which I did not fire because one has to be certain of a clean kill with only one shot at his disposal. After that, I took part in the last two days of the Massachusetts muzzle-loading deer season with equal lack of success. (Many states, including Massachusetts, have a muzzle-loading, or primitive weapon, deer season in addition to the one in which modern firearms may be used.)

The first creature to fall to my muzzle-loader this year was a varying hare in Vermont. With the hare—and two more given me by my hunting companions of that day—I journeyed to my married daughter's apartment in Amherst, Massachusetts, and while her husband was at work and she at her classes, I prepared them a rice and hasenpfeffer supper with panfried smelts, also from Vermont, as the first course. Both were well received, and that candlelit meal, for me at least, brought the wheel of life full circle.

Once celebrated in saga and song, often the most important man in the village, one upon whom many relied for sustenance and whom all young men strove to emulate, the hunter in America, now besieged by a vocal and often intelligent army of detractors, must, if he is at all sensitive, wonder if he is indeed an anachronism possessed by some madness that others have managed to throw off. And yet, he should also realize that over the centuries, the hunter has been more in tune with the natural world than most of his contemporaries.

In his remarkable book *The Hunting Hypothesis*, Robert Ardrey notes that man has been hunting for at least three million years, or 99 percent of his time on earth, and observes that "throughout that time natural selection accepted or discarded individuals or groups in terms of a single standard, our capacity to survive as hunters. Are we to believe, as so many victims of fashionable thought will assert, that such selection left no mark on us?"

Ardrey's postulate—which will disturb many readers—is that the basic elements of our nature "which we regard as so nobly our own ... sharing, cooperation, reponsibility, courage, self-sacrifice, loyalty," came into being because "we were meat-eating hunters."

Man's ability to use tools, to store information in writing, to stockpile food, and to manipulate his environment is at once his glory and his despair, for when he shifted from a hunter society to the agricultural-industrial age he began to insulate himself from this planet and to inflict damage on it. The leisure time gained gave birth to scientists, philosophers, painters, composers, musicians, and poets whose work certainly represents the rarest blend of intellect and soul, but with it came a despoiling industrial fury that has continued unabated.

Now the challenge for us (all arrogance and belief that science and technology can solve everything shed away) is to recognize that we only share earth with other living things and that its resources are finite.

Hunting, properly done, is not an outworn cruelty, but rather a manifestation of man's desire to reestablish or maintain a union with the natural world. There are various paths to this marriage, and those who wish to achieve it—whether hunters, naturalists or bird watchers—should join hands to preserve that which they seek to enter.

IN DEFENSE OF HUNTING[2]

Although the hunter, particularly if he is brought to bay at a Manhattan cocktail party, might feel that most people

[2] Article entitled "Study Sees Hunting Accepted," by Nelson Bryant, colunmnist. New York *Times*. Sec. 5, p 9:4. Mr. 9, '80. © 1980 by The New York Times Company. Reprinted by permission.

regard him as a nasty anachronism, a three-year study by Dr. Stephen Kellert, a Yale sociologist, reveals substantial nation-wide sentiment to the contrary.

The above finding is the first of our reports on the results of Dr. Kellert's endeavor—a survey of American attitudes toward wildlife—which was financed by a $450,000 grant from the United States Department of the Interior's Fish and Wildlife Service. All reports are scheduled to be completed by the end of this summer.

Dr. Kellert and his co-workers discovered that more than 80 percent of Americans approved of hunting for meat alone, whether subsistence hunting by Indians or Eskimos or meat hunting by others, most of whom do not seriously rely on hunting to provide food.

About 60 percent were opposed to hunting purely for sport and 85 percent were against so-called trophy hunting.

When asked if they approved of hunting for both meat and recreation, about 64 percent said yes.

Some 15 percent of those surveyed had hunted sometime during the previous two years, and 7 percent had hunted 11 times or more during that period. Nearly 25 percent said they had hunted at some point in their lives.

About 85 percent of those who hunt or had hunted were male.

More than half of those who had hunted at one time or another no longer do so. Asked why they stopped, 41 percent said they had no opportunity or time, 19 percent said that personal health intervened; another 19 percent said they had become opposed to hunting and 1.2 percent said they quit because a spouse objected.

Most of those who once hunted but now personally oppose it, Dr. Kellert said, do not object to others doing it.

There are significant numbers of Americans who feel that pleasure in the chase and kill is immoral and degrading; yet there are those, this writer among them, who feel that to hunt in cold-blooded, machine-like fashion would be infinitely worse, if indeed, there are any who could do so.

Every hunter is involved to some degree with the creature

he pursues, and when a kill does take place his mood varies from elation to sadness. As a hunter, I cannot explain this. I only know it is so.

I also know that as many hunters grow older, the urge to succeed softens, and someone who has been bringing home 70 waterfowl a season is content with a dozen and often not really disconsolate when he bags nothing. It is the ritual—with the possibility of success, however remote, to give it emotional substance—that sustains many old-time hunters, and there often comes a time when the guns are put away or given to grandchildren and hunting is done in memory.

This is not only the result of failing physical energy—most hunting is less demanding in this wise than tennis—but a growing awareness of the fragility of life.

At such a time the old hunter so moved does not feel that hunting is wrong, only that it is wrong for him.

There are some who hunt purely for sport, but they are, I believe, an insignificant minority. I base this observation on the hundreds of hunters I have known. Without the ceremony of preparing and eating the game, the endeavor dissolves into an immoral and worthless display of skill, or lack of it.

As noted, trophy hunting is held in high disfavor by most Americans. I am somewhat ambivalent on this subject. Personally I have no wish to adorn the walls of my house with horns or heads of animals I have shot and would rather remember them as they looked when alive.

But at the same time I am aware that many trophy hunters are men who have labored diligently on behalf of wildlife and who have often hunted so long that they have reached a stage wherein they will pass up shot after shot until the older, larger animal is before them. One might postulate that it is better to do this than to take a younger male of whatever species is being sought because the younger has more years of service to his kind ahead of him.

It should be also noted that few successful trophy hunts end with the head and cape, or skin, carted off and the carcass left behind as carrion.

As one might expect, attitudes toward hunting have pronounced demographic differences. Dr. Kellert discovered that 85 percent of those living in areas of under 500 population favored recreation-meat hunting, while only 46 percent in areas over one million supported the endeavor.

Dr. Kellert's work has not, as noted, been confined to hunting and has also examined, among other things, the public's attitude toward the financing of wildlife management such as hunters and fishermen are now doing through taxes on equipment and license fees. There was strong backing by the public for increased funds for such efforts through a sales tax on fur clothing (furs from wild animals), 82 percent; through entrance fees to public wildlife areas and wildlife refuges, 75 percent, and through a sales tax on off-road vehicles, such as snowmobiles and trail bikes, 71 percent. About 57 percent favored taxes on backpacking and camping equipment, and 54 percent felt that birdwatching equipment should be included. Fifty-seven percent also supported the idea of increased general tax revenues for wildlife management.

Surprisingly a majority of those interviewed felt that wildlife and wildlife habitats should be protected at the expense of jobs or housing. Two-thirds of those questioned—including 77 percent of the Alaskans—said they would be opposed to oil development in Yellowstone National Park if it would harm the park's wildlife.

As a group, Alaskans showed a greater knowledge of wildlife than did the residents of any other area and were highly supportive of measures—even if they involved economic hardship—to protect it. At the same time, they have fewer emotional or sentimental notions about animals. To quote the report:

"Thus, while Alaskans appear knowledgeable, ecologically informed and highly protective toward wildlife and natural habitat, this concern was not correlated with any moralistic objection to consumptive wildlife use, nor overly emotional attachments to animals."

Lynn A. Greenwalt, director of the Fish and Wildlife Service, has observed that while wildlife management can never be a popularity contest, Dr. Kellert's report will help in establishing broad policy guidelines and will provide "further understanding of the public's need for greater awareness and education on wildlife matters."

CONGRESS TAKES AIM AT PET POPULATION EXPLOSION[3]

The pet population explosion that threatens to engulf the country may be halted by a stop sign that has been raised by Congress.

For years, the number of pets—primarily dogs and cats— has been skyrocketing. The boom led to animal-breeding practices that further escalated the problem.

America's 215 million people own some 100 million cats and dogs. That is the highest ratio of pets to people for any nation, including animal-loving Britain, where the ratio is 1 to 3.

One study indicates that since 1965, the dog population has increased by 4.5 percent a year. At that rate, the number of dogs would double in 15.4 years.

Now, under terms of a newly enacted law, sanctions against indiscriminate transportation and selling of pets have been strengthened. This is expected to limit the sale of animals, particularly of diseased or mistreated pets.

But the problem is enormous.

"Throwaway" Pets

Since Americans now "dispose" of about 20 million dogs and cats annually, it seems clear that the supply exceeds the demand—that animals are a part of a "throwaway society." The control of animals, including destruction of 13 million

---

[3] Article entitled "100 Million Dogs and Cats; Congress Takes Aim At Pet Population Explosion," by the news staff. *U.S. News & World Report.* 81:48-9. Jl. 26, '76. Copyright 1976 U.S. News & World Report, Inc. Reprinted with permission.

pets by municipal pounds, is a 500-million-dollar annual burden on taxpayers.

Of the unwanted animals, about 5 million roam free. They live an average of about 2½ years before dying of disease or starvation or under the wheels of a car. Only one abandoned animal in 10 finds a new home.

The problem of the free-roaming animals is not to be taken lightly, authorities warn. Dogs and cats can carry 65 diseases transmittable to man, and 40 of those diseases have been identified in the U.S. Aside from the disease aspect about 1.5 million Americans require medical treatment for dog bites each year, and approximately 30,000 have to undergo rabies treatment.

Moreover, only about half of the bites incurred are reported. Of the people bitten, 75 percent are under age 20.

One expert on the pet population is Prof. Lloyd C. Faulkner, chairman of the department of physiology and biophysics at Colorado State University. He assesses the situation this way: "The pet problem is like an overflowing bathtub with the drain open but with the tap running full force."

Commercial Breeders

Causes of the tremendous upsurge in pet population figures are many and varied.

Puppies are being produced by the millions on an assembly-line basis, chiefly in the Midwest. Breeders find ready buyers among the country's 10,000 or more pet shops.

Thousands of weak and undernourished pups, many already diseased, are sold across the nation.

Some of these young animals are accompanied by fraudulent certificates of health that have been provided by unscrupulous veterinarians, according to animal-welfare workers.

The U.S. Department of Agriculture, which licenses certain pet breeders and dealers under the Animal Welfare Act of 1970, has been accused of failure to enforce its own standards.

Franz L. Dantzler, director of field service and investigations for the Humane Society of the U.S., says that at least half of the breeders licensed by the USDA's Animal and Plant Health Inspection Service—APHIS—do not meet the agency's standards.

Few Breeding Curbs

In the U.S., which already has about 45 million dogs and 55 million cats, plus numerous other species of animals, there have been few effective curbs on the breeding of pets for sale.

Aside from the 5,133 breeders and dealers who are licensed by APHIS, there are estimated to be about 100,000 unlicensed, part-time commercial breeders in the U.S.

It is not unusual for large breeders to ship as many as 3,000 puppies a year. The trade in kittens is far less extensive, since cats are prolific breeders and thousands are simply given away.

All this involves big money for pet owners and taxpayers in general. The breeding, care, feeding and grooming of dogs and cats is a 3.9-billion-dollar industry, according to the trade publication *Pets/Supplies/Marketing.*

Household pets often are merchandised in much the same way as Detroit's autos—and scrapped in similar fashion.

Income for dog breeders ranges from a few hundred dollars a year for the backyard breeder to more than $250,000 for the big kennel owner.

Dog breeding can be generally profitable all around. A toy poodle sold by a Missouri breeder for $50 may retail in a pet shop for $130 to $150. A Doberman that changed hands in Kansas for $75 might bring $250 at a Washington, D.C., pet shop.

To achieve maximum profit, it is not uncommon for many breeders to wean pups at three weeks and ship them out one week later.

These prematurely weaned animals often suffer dietary deficiencies and rarely attain full growth. Some are so traumatized by the experience that they develop antisocial traits and will never make good pets.

Frustrated Concern

About the only controls over breeders are license requirements, anti-cruelty statutes, state sanitation laws and transport regulations. Humane Society workers say that complaints about filthy kennels and inhumane practices,
especially in transportation, are mostly an operation in futil-
ity.

Because of the lax controls, thousands of pups that are
wormy or diseased, or both, are shipped in interstate commerce. It is this practice that the new law is aimed at termi-
nating.

Fay Brisk, animal-welfare consultant in Washington,
D.C., estimates that during a three-year period, approximately 20,000 puppies arrived at one of the capital's air-cargo
terminals from the Midwest, and that one third of them were
afflicted by worms or disease. Many arrived dead.

A veterinarian in Greensboro, N.C., reported to the Humane Society of the U.S. that he examined several hundred
pups shipped to a pet store. He said 50 percent of them suffered from distemper and died within five days. All came
from the Midwest.

Four Midwestern states— Missouri, Kansas, Iowa and Ne-
braska—are the chief suppliers for pet stores. Of the 5,131
dealers licensed by APHIS, 3,141 are located in these states.
No laws that could be applied to breeding of pets exist there,
says the Humane Society. The American Kennel Club estimates that puppy breeding in the four states is a 40-million-
dollar business.

All but four states—Ohio, Pennsylvania, Maine and Hawaii—have laws which require that pets arriving in their
jurisdictions have health certificates. But the Humane Society
says the laws are rarely enforced.

Some breeders defeat the health-certificate requirements,
the Society says, by persuading friendly veterinarians to
sign stacks of blank certificates that can be completed as
needed.

Help on Way

Under pressure from consumer groups and local humane societies, some first steps have been taken by state governments to improve the conditions under which household pets are bred and shipped.

To discourage the transportation of undernourished and weak puppies, Connecticut, Maryland, California and New York forbid the shipment across their borders of pups under 8 weeks, unless accompanied by their dams.

New York also has a "defective merchandise" law under which pet shops selling sick pups must offer refunds.

In 1973, Illinois adopted its own animal-welfare act. It applies to all pet shops and breeders except those producing fewer than six litters a year.

Dr. David Bromwell, a veterinarian charged with administering the Illinois law, says his office resolves about 2,500 complaints annually, mostly involving sick or unsatisfactory pets.

Illinois requires a pet seller to accept return of an animal within 48 hours if the buyer has a reasonable complaint. If a veterinarian finds a pet diseased, the seller must pay the medical bill. The seller also can offer a refund or provide a substitute pet.

Fred Moberley, owner of Petland, one of Chicago's largest pet retailers, says he welcomes the new law because he believes it has improved the image of the business and led to the closing of inhumane pet shops.

Floyd Clark, a large kennel operator in Barnes, Kans., has formed the National Pet Dealers and Breeders Association. The group, with 200 members, has as its objective the upgrading of conditions under which dogs are bred and sold in the U.S.

A source of irritation to a good many people connected with humane societies and to breeders like Mr. Clark and officials such as Mr. Bromwell is the inspection agency APHIS.

Although the organization made more than 38,000 inspections and searches in 1974 under the old Animal Welfare

Act, it revoked just one license. Dr. Pierre Chaloux, an APHIS official, asserts that the service's 2,000 inspectors are able to spend less than 5 percent of their time making inspections because of the burden of other duties.

"What we have been trying to do instead of revoking licenses is to get people in compliance," explains Dr. Chaloux.

But Dr. Bromwell criticizes this attitude. He says that he notifies APHIS when he finds a licensed kennel that is not in compliance with federal regulations, but nothing happens. And he asks: "How do you get them off their duffs?"

Reprinted from U.S. News & World Report.

"BEST FRIEND" BEST THERAPY?[4]

At the University of Maryland Hospital in Baltimore not long ago, 64 men and 28 women became the subjects of a study that was to upset the notions of many physicians.

All had been hospitalized because of heart attack or severe chest pain, indicating serious heart disease. All recovered after treatment in intensive-care units and in time went home.

But while in the hospital, all had been studied intensively not just in terms of their disease. Dr. Erika Friedmann and other investigators had made a special study of factors in the patients' lives—environmental stress, economic status, social contacts, and others which might have any influence on the course of their illness.

One factor stood out: of the 92 patients, 39 did not own pets. Within a year of their hospital admission, 11 of these patients had died. In contrast, all but three of the 53 pet owners were alive at the end of the year.

The findings, as the *Journal of the American Medical Association* notes, "fly in the face of the advice given by some physicians to dispose of pets because they might be an unneces-

[4] Article by Lawrence Galton, freelance writer. *Parade Magazine.* p 20. Je. 3, '79.

sary burden." On the basis of her study, Dr. Friedmann has urged that "pet ownership should be investigated as a therapeutic tool."

Recently the recuperative effects of pets have been coming in for increasing study. And the gratifying, even somewhat astonishing findings have application to problems other than heart trouble.

In Britain, for example, investigators set out to determine the effects of pets on social attitudes and mental and physical health in people aged 75 to 81. Some of the subjects, who lived alone in an urban area of Hull, East Yorkshire, were given budgerigars because the small, colorful birds are easy to care for.

Several study groups were set up. Groups 1 and 2 owned TV sets; groups 3 and 4 did not. The investigators expected that a pet might be less significant in the life of an older person who owned a TV set than one who did not, but they wanted to find out definitely through comparison.

Members of groups 1 and 3 were given budgerigars, and those in groups 2 and 4 received begonia house plants.

The presence of the birds made a consistent, significant difference in the lives of the study subjects, while the presence or absence of TV sets had no detectable effect.

Not only was there a surprisingly intimate attachment to the birds, but investigators "found in our visits that they had become such a powerful tool for conversation that they could even displace the monotonous awareness and discussion of past and pending medical ailments."

In the U.S., Dr. Samuel A. Corson and his colleagues at the Ohio State University Department of Psychiatry, Columbus, have been exploring "pet-facilitated psychotherapy" in a psychiatric hospital and a nursing home.

These studies began almost fortuitously. Corson had set out to observe the effects of stress on dogs, hoping to gain insights into the effects on humans. A "dog ward" was established at the Ohio State University Psychiatric Hospital.

Some patients, especially adolescents who had been uncommunicative throughout their hospital stay, began to ask to play with or help take care of the dogs.

So the Corson team began to plan a study. They chose 50 of the most seriously ill patients, who had not responded to traditional forms of psychiatric treatment.

Animals from the "dog ward" were introduced to the patients—in the kennels, on the patient ward, even to patients who spent most of their time in bed.

Only three refused to accept a dog. All the others soon were showing a degree of improvement—in some cases, remarkable improvement.

Sonny, a 19-year-old psychotic, had spent almost all of his time lying in bed, barring all efforts of the staff to get him to move about. He refused to participate in occupational, recreational or group therapy, did not respond to drugs. Before scheduled shock therapy was started, a wirehair fox terrier named Arwyn was brought to Sonny.

What followed astonished the researchers. Sonny tumbled the dog about joyously, asked where he could keep her, followed her when she jumped to the floor. He soon opened up to therapy and to other patients, later recovered and was discharged.

Marsha, a 23-year-old licensed practical nurse had been brought to the hospital disoriented, shouting "destroy the world." Diagnosis: catatonic schizophrenia. Drug treatment failed to help. Electroshock—25 sessions of it—did no good. She had become increasingly withdrawn, frozen, almost mute.

For the first few hours after being given a dog, she remained withdrawn. But then she began to communicate with the dog; and when the pet was taken away, she went after it. Before long she was walking and stroking the dog and soon communicating with other patients about the pet. Later she, too, was discharged.

Despite the program's success, it had to be stopped. Research funds ran out; the dog colony had to be disbanded. However, the Castle Nursing Homes in Millersburg, Ohio, took most of the dogs and carried on research.

There the pets were welcomed by the elderly residents, many of them bedridden or in wheelchairs. Well-trained wirehair fox terriers and small poodles (miniatures, teacups) proved to be especially appealing to love-hungry, depressed, withdrawn residents and those with low mobility.

"These dogs," report the researchers, "with their resilience, aggressive friendliness, good humor, and playfulness, served as effective ice-breakers and social matchmakers."

"Use of pets," says Dr. Corson, "is not a cure but rather a facilitator. It doesn't cure old age, but we think it can bring these patients out emotionally so they think better of themselves and interact more effectively with others. And it can bring them out physically because they often begin to romp or walk with the dog."

Pet-facilitated psychotherapy is still in its early stages. More research is needed on selecting and training appropriate dogs or other pets to meet particular needs of patients in mental health hospitals or other custodial institutions, including nursing homes—and, possibly, Dr. Corson says, some penal institutions as well.

"Eventually," he says, "we would like to have a properly funded research and training program for pet animals and therapists to develop Feeling Heart dogs to do for mental health programs what Seeing Eye dogs do for the blind."

THEY'VE FINALLY GOT AN EDGE![5]

There is a horse-scent in the morning air, sharp as wood smoke or any other natural thing, and the horses stamp and whinny in their stalls at the Rock Creek Horse Centre in Washington, D.C. Bob Douglas, owner, ringmaster, stable inspector, and all-around prime mover at the center, sits at his desk, his big hands on the arms of the chair and his crutches beside him. At the time he bought the stables, he was totally blind and in a wheelchair. Roughly six months after that his

[5] Article by Judith Shepard Rosenfeld, freelance writer in the Washington, D.C. area. *American Education*. 15:20-6. My. '79. Published by the U.S. Department of Health, Education and Welfare. USGPO.

sight came back, but he was still in a wheelchair. Reason: multiple sclerosis.

"If I had been functional, I would have stayed on in the Public Health Service and operated the stable as a sideline," he says. "But retiring from the National Institutes of Health put me here full time. One day I started riding again, not so much for physical therapy as for my own ego. The psychological effects of riding so increased my self-esteem that I was able to say to myself and believe it, 'Everything isn't lost.' Then the idea came to me: If it's good for me, it has to be good for other people, too."

The test of that idea arrived soon after in the person of a small girl in a big helmet. She was one of a class of handicapped children invited by Douglas for a ride at the center. She was six years old, her name was Stephanie, and she wore the helmet 24 hours a day because she suffered from the spasticity of cerebral palsy and fell down a lot. Supported by two people, she was helped to the riding ring, where a pony named Pickles was waiting for her. On hand as riding instructor was Jean McCally, holder of a degree in psychological counseling and a firm belief in the value of riding as therapy. She helped to hoist the aimlessly thrashing child onto Pickles's back.

"She was a kid. I'm a lover of kids," Bob Douglas says. "It didn't matter whether she could walk or not, or whether she had to wear a helmet all the time. After we managed to get her on top of the pony, all of a sudden this huge smile flashed across her face.

"When she got off, I told her mother that I thought Stephanie was interested in horses, and maybe just being up on one would help psychologically anyway. Her mother agreed to that and gave me the name of her doctor and her physiotherapist. They told me 'We don't think riding lessons will help anybody, but if you think it will, do it.' So Stephanie was our first student."

Stephanie's lessons with McCally started in November of 1972. By February of the following year, Stephanie, with the

approval of her medical advisors, was wearing her helmet
only while she was on horseback.

She was getting the same sort of physical therapy she used
to get in an office," Douglas says, "but on the table it had
been 'Stretch your right leg as far as you can' or 'Take your
right hand and touch your left toes.' And, actually, what Stephanie did on a horse wasn't any different from what a physically able person would do when riding. The basics involve
learning to balance the body and, for people with physical
problems, just being able to balance is a hard chore. We
worked on Stephanie's balance, teaching her how to shift her
weight, how to put her weight in her legs, working with the
muscles in her back. The difference was that she was more
interested in doing it on a horse than on a table."

With Stephanie's physical improvement, there were
other, equally exciting developments.

"She wasn't only walking better," Douglas recalls, "she
was more outgoing. Her personality changed. She remembered the days when she had riding lessons. She remembered
the name of her horse. She remembered *all* the important
things in her life. Her schoolwork got better. There was a dis-
tinct carry-over from stable to classroom, and this made me
decide to look at riding not only for physically handicapped
kids, but for kids with mental problems, learning disabilities,
and what-have-you."

And so the next stage of Bob Douglas's idea emerged: "If
riding could improve Stephanie's schoolwork, then it could
work with any youngster."

It was an idea ahead of its time. Douglas remembers the
next months with scant pleasure. He and Jean McCally
scoured the area for funds but the answer was always the
same: There was no money available to heal children
through riding.

"That's a very easy thing to say, 'No money available,' "
Douglas says without any visible bitterness, "but I think that
what goes on underneath is that most people are afraid of
horses. While they say 'no money,' they really think, 'If I'm
afraid, then so's a six-year-old child who can't walk or who is

retarded. Horses are dangerous, they step on you, they bite you, they kick you.' All of this is a turn-off.

"Then, of course, the other suspicion they have is that I've come in with a new boondoggle."

For months, McCally and Douglas looked for money with no success. Douglas is matter-of-fact about what happened next.

"In September of 1973, we decided that if the D.C. public schools could furnish transportation for 35 handicapped young students—mentally retarded, learning-disabled, emotionally disturbed, and physically handicapped children—we would provide the service free. There was a twofold reason: First, I knew, even on the basis of only two people—myself and Stephanie—that it would work. Second, I really wanted to get involved with the kids, and if we had to do it for nothing—okay. The school system was perfectly willing to provide the students, as long as there was no price tag on the service. We said, 'Fine, you give us the kids.' "

Douglas took ten students from a school for educable mentally retarded children, ten from a school for trainable mentally retarded young people whose education stresses life skills first and the three Rs second. There were physically handicapped children from a third school. And there were ten emotionally disturbed boys, aged 12 to 18, from a closed educational institution.

Of the last group, Douglas says, "These are kids who have been through a great emotional crisis in their lives. They may have seen their mother's boyfriend kill the mother. They may themselves have done something similar. They've been removed from the system, put into closed educational city institutions instead of sent to reform school. They are called 'residential' kids."

The first handicapped students ranged in age from four to 35, mental retardation not being judged by chronological age. Four, Douglas admits, is a bit young. "We don't normally accept four-year-olds at the stable, but I make exceptions with our handicapped kids because I feel what they are going through. I teach them myself whenever I can, and I feel good about doing it. It's very difficult to impose on someone to teach a disabled person something without that someone being either trained or emotionally involved in the situation. The program, even now, requires special instructors, but at the beginning there were just the two of us—Jean and myself—and, of course, 35 students."

It was, Douglas says now, a near disaster. He was then, as he is today, opposed to "mixing students," placing mentally slow children with physically handicapped ones, or either group with emotionally disturbed students because, he knows, even handicapped children tend to stare at the unfamiliar.

Says Douglas, "Even though they never say that they know they're labeled, they know that there's something different about them. If they're going to have a lot of strangers—even if the strangers are fellow students—staring at them, they're right back in the same ball park. 'Why are those people staring at me? Something has to be wrong with me!' they'll think, instead of 'I'm here at the stable, and I'm doing something on my own, and everybody's trying to help me.' "

That sensitivity to the feelings of his first handicapped students is what led to the moment when Douglas found himself, for the first time, in a riding ring facing an unmixed phalanx of ten disturbed boys who routinely spent their days in a locked institution because of histories filled with fear and violence. He shakes his head, remembering.

"Even though we had all these ideas in the back of our minds—what we were going to do and how we were going to succeed—we still didn't know what we were getting into. These kids were hardcore cases. We had talked to them about horses. We gave them the rules they should follow. We told them that they should stick to the rules and that they should help one another. That was the basic thing, helping one another.

"They had a chance to get the feel of a horse and to get on top and be led around maybe once. But they simply were not used to having someone explain how things should be done. Their feeling was 'I'm not interested in protecting my buddy.

I'd just as soon have my horse run over him as anything else.'
Some would kick the horse, or smack him. And I really
couldn't control them. They were completely out of control,
totally out of control.

"They were here for two hours. After they'd gone, I called
Jean into the office and told her, 'I'm not really sure I want to
do this. They're going to wreck themselves and they're going
to wreck everything,' There was no feeling of love, no sympathy."

Saddened and deeply upset, the two sat and talked for a
long time and finally they agreed to give it one more try.

The next week, the ten were back.

"Same faces," Douglas says in remembered awe, "and *entirely different personalities.* Unbelievable. It was enough to
make you cry . . . just a complete change. It made me see that,
no matter what, the program was going to work."

Douglas doesn't know what happened in that week, but
he believes that those ten youngsters came around to realizing that someone was trying to help them. "I think the biggest
thing that's lacking with kids with really severe emotional
problems is love. They're hard to love. And being hard to love
makes it hard for them to give love."

One of the more difficult boys of those first days asked
Douglas whether he had fallen off a horse or had been kicked
by one. Douglas told him he had multiple sclerosis and asked,
"Do you know what that is?"

The youngster answered, "Yeah, I've seen it on TV." And
then he said, "It kills you."

When Douglas told the boy that sometimes it does, the
boy said, "Since you know that you are going to die, why are
you helping me?"

Says Douglas, "I guess what he was saying was, 'I have
problems, but your problems are worse than mine. So why are
you involving yourself with me?' I told him, 'I'm helping you
so you can help someone else.' "

Among those hard-to-love boys in the first five-month riding program, Douglas says, there was a carry-over from week
to week of the message that loving care without the use of

force is what counts, not a rough, bitter approach. For those youngsters, it was a revelation to discover they could master a thousand-pound animal—control him without force, but with love and care.

Whether or not that period also put the parents on the right track is another question. The fact is that four or five parents started coming out to the riding lessons. "The students were actually forcing them to come," says Douglas. "I think this was the key to the whole thing. The kids were saying, 'I'm finally doing something and you've got to see it.'"

With the retarded and physically handicapped children in the first program, Douglas reports a similar growth of communication between teachers and students and between students and other children in the neighborhood. "They are easier to handle," he says, "and there is a rise in self-esteem and a new confidence that can be seen right away. The kids who ride here have something to carry back, not only to their classmates at school but to other children in their neighborhoods. It's as if they're saying, 'I'm doing something you're not doing and I'm going to tell you all about it, and I want you to get a little jealous of it.' It's an edge. They've finally got an edge!"

The first sign of a breakthrough according to Douglas, is volubility. Lonely children who have been locked into silence begin to talk.

Douglas believes that language can be a clue to a problem with children. They can refuse to express themselves, just refuse to talk. "This isn't true only of those who are handicapped," he says, "it's true of practically all youngsters. What they're saying is, 'I'd rather not talk if I don't have anything to talk about.' Here at the stable, children are getting something to talk about, and they start to talk and force people to talk to them, to listen, and to respond. Back in the classroom there's the terrific experience of asking 'What color is a pinto?' and having a retarded child burst forth with the answer, being able to say. 'Hey! Listen to me. I know something!'"

With that sort of result as the spur, Douglas was determined to keep the riding program going after the first five months, even though expenses were mounting. "Even now," he says staunchly, "if we had to do it for nothing, we would, except that you just can't operate very long doing things for zero. It was costing us a great deal of money, about ten thousand dollars for the first half of the school year."

Salvation came from the National Capital Park Service, a division of the U.S. Department of the Interior, which is reponsible for the huge and beautiful wooded tract in which the stable operates as a concession. Park Service director "Jud" Fish was willing to sponsor the children for the rest of the school year as a park activity. The following September, the National Park Service allocated $20,000 with which Douglas continued the program for 35 different children.

By then Douglas and McCally had discovered a key to the kind of teaching in which they were engaged: mastery. There are many facets to mastery in riding, Douglas feels. One is mastery of the fear of horses; another is control of the animal. When a child can respond successfully to an order to bring the horse he or she is riding to a stop, the mastering point has been reached. The teacher and a student who may have trouble completing any task have completed a whole cycle. "When I speak about mastering," Douglas tells the students, "I speak about being able to follow any given thing to completion and to know that I have completed that task for you and for myself."

The children were gaining mastery and carrying new skills and new confidence back to their classrooms. Douglas saw this happening, but he also saw that something was lacking. It wasn't that the students did not want to learn, but that the teacher was not able to teach. "We decided to teach teachers, too," he says. "Not to ride horses, although they could if they wanted to, but how to teach the child. And teachers welcomed it. What was happening was that the children were asking the teachers, 'What is a bridle? What is a bit?' And the teacher, all of a sudden, didn't know more than the child, whose whole approach was changing to wanting to know."

So Douglas, helped by his wife, Dorothy, who was trained in special education, went to work on the teachers and the results were not long in coming. First was the rapid descent of the teachers from their pedestals. The children saw that the teachers had the same fear they had. One boy said of his teacher, "I'm afraid to go on that horse, but she's afraid to go on that horse, too."

"With handicapped and retarded kids," says Douglas, "the distance between student and teacher is so great that it's hard for a kid to communicate with the teacher. But every time they come back here, that distance is a little less. The experience brought the monuments down and the communication just got bigger."

Another result was that inventive teachers were giving newly eager children arithmetic problems involving horses, pictures of pintos to color, drawings of hooves and pasterns and bridles and girths to identify. One room of educable retarded children embarked on a study of California through association of the colors of the palomino horse—gold and yellow—with the history, landscape, and climate of that state.

Triumphantly, the Douglases took transcripts of a preliminary study of the academic value of the program to the National Capital Park Service, where they were told that the educational character of the program now made it the responsibility of the school system, though the Park Service would certainly continue to permit use of the federally owned land for the program. It was the right moment. Vincent Reed, who had just been appointed superintendent of schools in Washington, took over the funding of the Rock Creek Horse Centre Program under the aegis of the school system's special education section. It was fortuitous but not an unmixed blessing. The program is now dividing its limited funds among 400 students, each of whom has a scantier share of the hours that the stables and the four ever-patient instructors can give.

The years of effort are now starting to bear fruit. Douglas is gaining recognition in the capital city for his stubborn, visionary fight for handiapped children. Colman McCarthy, columnist for the Washington *Post* and an old friend of the riding venture, wrote of Douglas: "The Rock Creek Horse Centre is a little piece of earth, of which Robert Douglas is the salt. . . . In exposing children to the simple mysteries of horsemanship, he has seen their lives transformed by a thirst to learn about some of life's more complex mysteries, like reading and writing. . . .

Just how triumphantly the simple mysteries have been co-opted by Douglas's larger dream of mastery for afflicted children is shown in a study by the Special Education Learning Centers from whom Douglas draws many of his students. The study evaluated the effect of the Therapeutic Riding Program on students described as "mild to moderate exceptional students," or educably retarded children. While there were areas in which the program was shown to have little or no effect upon the children, there were other areas in which it scored impressively:

—Listening skills and the ability to follow instructions are up 80 percent.

—Interest in learning rose by 41 percent.

—Self-confidence was 62 percent higher.

—Physical orientation, or the ability to tell up from down, left from right, near from far, rose by about 60 percent.

And, loud and clear, the voices of silent children were being heard for the first time in the classroom. Opposite "verbalizing needs," the report read: "93 percent improved." The same for the ability to "relate a brief incident." Experience-sharing was up 91 percent; 76 percent more children were using and retaining new vocabulary, 80 percent were added to the number using whole sentences.

One teacher whose children completed the course writes: "Throughout the entire program, I could see something developing which was carried from the stable to the classroom and vice versa: accountability. Each student had become accountable for his behavior, his horse's behavior, and even the instructor's behavior. . . . Our only regret is that we cannot have an ongoing stable activity to look forward to, now that we have learned to groom and ride the horses. Of course, we can carry on the games, the reading and math lessons in our classroom and at home, but to see Big Mac, Parfait, Merilene, Coffee Cake and the other horses again—it is a dream yet to come true."

"I dream, too," Douglas says. "I look across the riding rings into the woods on the other side and I think of all the portable classrooms this city has stacked up and unused, and I imagine a semi-circle of little white buildings over there. I have fantasies of a whole school built around riding for these children, with all the growth and the skills we could give them."

Something like that could yet happen. Washington's new city administration has begun exploring the possibilities in conjunction with the Interior Department. At the same time, some of Douglas's supporters in the metropolitan area are proceeding with plans to set up a "therapeutic riding foundation" to help children who, either because they live outside the District limits or go to private schools, are not covered by the D.C. public school program. Part of the planned program envisions a series of pilot studies comparing the achievements of full-time students in the same academic curriculum but different riding schedules—from every day to twice a week.

Douglas, who is now 45, spent 17 years at the National Institutes of Health as a virologist before illness forced his retirement. With three other scientists he developed a vaccine against rubella, or German measles, an otherwise trivial disease which, in pregnant women, was responsible for a tragic number of handicapped babies. "I still feel very good about that," Douglas says. "But right here, the horse center, this program, this is the best thing I've ever done. This is what it's all about."

BIBLIOGRAPHY

* An asterisk (°) preceding a reference imdicates that the article or part of it has been reprinted in this book.

BOOKS AND PAMPHLETS

Adams, Charles C. Guide to the study of animal ecology. Arno Press. '78.

Amory, Cleveland. Man kind? Our incredible war on wildlife. Harper. '74.

Ardrey, Robert. The hunting hypothesis; a personal conclusion concerning the evolutionary nature of man. Atheneum. '76

Bixby, William. Of animals and men; a comparison of human and animal behavior. McKay. '68.

Bleibtreu, John N. The parable of the beast. Macmillan. '67.

Bokun, Branko. Man: the fallen ape. Doubleday. '77.

Bowman, John C. Animals for man. Edward Arnold, Ltd., London. '77.

Carson, Gerald. Men, beasts, and gods: a history of cruelty and kindness to animals. Scribner. '72.

Caver, Mavis and Hutchings, Monica. Man's dominion: our violation of the animal world. Rupert Hart-Davis. '70.

Cochrane, Brian M. Your pets, your health, and the law. Wiley. '79.

Curtis, Patricia. Animal rights. Four Winds. '80.

Davis, Flora. Eloquent animals. Putnam, '78.

Dewsbury, Donald. Comparative animal behavior. McGraw-Hill. '78.

Domalain, Jean Yves. The animal connection; the confessions of an ex-wild animal trafficker. Morrow. '77.

Eiseley, Loren. The invisible pyramid. Scribner. '72.

Fox, Michael W. Between animal and man, Blond and Briggs. '77.

Fox, M. W. and Morris R. K., eds. On the fifth day: animal rights and human ethics. Acropolis Books. '78.

Frost, Sir Sydney. The whaling question (the Report of the Inquiry into Whales and Whaling). Friends of the Earth. '79.

Godlovitch, Stanley and Roslind, and Harris, John. Animals, men and morals: an enquiry into the maltreatment of non-humans. Taplinger. '72.

Hahn, Emily. On the side of the apes. Crowell. '71.

Haverstock, M. S. An American bestiary. Abrams. '79.

Klaits, Joseph and Barrie, eds. Animals and man in historical perspective. Harper. '74.

Krutch, J. W. The great chain of life. Houghton. '57.

Leavitt, E. S. Animals and their legal rights, a survey of American laws from 1641 to 1968. Animal Welfare Institute. Box 3650, Washington, D.C. 20007. '78.

√ Linzey, Andrew. Animal rights: a Christian assessment of man's treatment of animals. SCM Press, Ltd., London. '76.

Lockley, Ronald M. Whales, dolphins, and porpoises. Norton. '80.

Lorenz, Konrad. On aggression. Harcourt. '63.

Lubow, Robert. The war animals. Doubleday. '77.

√ McCoy, J. J. In defense of animals. Seabury Press. '78.

Myers, Norman. The sinking ark: a new look at the problem of disappearing species. Pergamon. '79.

Nowell, Iris. The dog crisis. St. Martin's Press. '78.

Paterson, David and Ryder, Richard, eds. Animals' rights; a symposium. Centaur Press. '79.

Peng, Fred C. C., ed. Sign language and language acquisition in man and ape. Westview Press. '78.

Pommery, Jean. How human the animals. Stein & Day. '77.

Rensberger, Boyce. The cult of the wild. Anchor Press. '77.

Richelle, M. and Helga Lejeune. Time in animal behavior. Pergamon. '80.

Ryder, R. D. Victims of science: the use of animals in research. Davis-Poynter, London. '75.

Sebeok, T. A., ed. How animals communicate. Indiana University Press. '77.

Shepard, Paul. Thinking animals: animals and the development of human intelligence. Viking. '78.

√ Singer, Peter. Animal liberation: a new ethics for our treatment of animals. Avon. '77.

Vyvyan, John. In pity and in anger; a study of the use of animals in science. Transatlantic. '72.

Williams, Leonard. Challenge to survival. Harper & Row. '77.

Zuber, Christian. Animals in danger. Barrons Eductional. '78.

PERIODICALS

*American Education. 15:26–6. My. '79. They've finally got an edge! Judith S. Rosenfeld.

Atlantic Monthly. 237:100–2. Mr. '76. Why the tortoise is kind and other tales of sociobiology. Frederick Hapgood.

*Atlantic Monthly. 238:58–65. S. '76. Lo, the poor animals! What did Noah save them for? James Fallows.

*Atlantic Monthly. 240:66–70. D. '77. Behold the hunter. Nelson Bryant.

Atlas. 25:44. Jl. '78. Do animals have rights? Nergis Dalal.

Audubon. 79:121–5. My. '77. Mighty, like a Furbish lousewort. Peter Steinhart.

Audubon. 80:221–4. Ja. '78. Pest control: Parasites in search of friends. Frank Graham Jr.

Audubon. 80:8–13. Mr. '78. Elephants on the beach. Irene Brady.

Audubon. 82:5–6+. Ja. '80. Porpoises resurface. Robert Cahn.

Audubon. 82:80–97. Ja. '80. Bitter harvest: hunting in America. J. G. Mitchell.

BioScience. 26:735. D. '76. Primates: conservation through research. R. D. Hunt.

BioScience. 28:148. F. '78. Laboratories must abide by NIH animal care rules.

BioScience. 28:409–10. Je. '78. Researchers concerned about changes in animal care policy. N. K. Eskridge.

BioScience. 29:145–8+. Mr. '79. Stress science, not ethics—animal experimentation: the battle lines soften. R. M. Henig.

BioScience. 29:651–3. N. '79. Animal welfare groups press for limits on high school research. R. M. Henig.

Christianity Today. 22:38–9. F. 10, '78. Christians and animals. J. R. W. Stott.

Commonweal. 106:39–41. F. 2, '79. On killing a deer. Thomas Powers.

Education Digest. 43:60–1. S. '77. Humane education: a forgotten mandate. P. J. Quinn.

Environment. 19:6–15. O. '77. The Endangered Species Act. Kevin Shea.

Environment. 21:5+. Ja. '79. Regulating trade in animals and plants. E. A. Goldstein.

Environment. 21:28–31. O. '79. Impact of Canine Clean-up Law; New York City. A. M. Beck.

FDA Consumer. 12:3. My. '78. Cooperation set on animal test rules; FDA-EPA agreement.

Field & Stream. 79:10+. Ap. '75. Hunters: the endangered species. E. B. Mann.

Futurist. 14:76. F. '80. Endangered species: the price of survival.

Gerontologist. 19:368–72. Ag. '79. Therapeutic roles of cat mascots with a hospital-based geriatric population: a staff survey. C. M. Brickel.

*Harper's. 252:3. Mr. '76. People and animals: the uneasy entente. Richard Adams.

*Harper's. 252:4. Mr. '76. Biological imperialism. Samuel Bleecker.

Harper's. 252:121. Mr. '76. How animals make you sick. M. H. Milts.

Human Behavior. 8:24. F. '79. Fido as shrink.

°International Wildlife. 7:36–9. S. '77. If pandas scream ... an earthquake is coming! Phylis Magida.

International Wildlife. 8:16+. My. '78. Chimp that went fishing: animals that use tools. Ivor Smullen.

International Wildlife. 9:1–56. S. '79. Special issue: Animal behavior.

International Wildlife. 9:46–51. S. '79. Man's view of the other animals. Peter Gwynne.

°Los Angeles Times. p N3. O. 22, '78. Wildlife is moving into the cities. Robert C. Toth.

McCalls. 104:88+. F. '77. Why animals develop emotional problems. M. W. Fox.

Ms. Magazine. 6:65–7. Ja. '78. Law of the jungle (revised): do you know that the king of beasts is a permissive father? Cynthia Moss.

National Geographic. 155:506–41. Ap. '79. Trouble with dolphins. E. J. Linehan.

National Wildlife. 17:32–9. O. '79. Crackdown on animal smuggling. Sam Iker.

Nation's Business. 66:11–12. Ag. '78. Lessons to be learned from a bad law. Supreme Court's opinion on the Tellico Dam and endangered species act. J. J. Kilpatrick.

Natural History. 86:78–82+. Je. '77. Lorenz observed. G. E. Allen.

Natural History. 86:84+. Ag. '77. Bambi factor; animal symbolism. Bernard Nietschmann.

Natural History. 86:20+. D. '77. Caring groups and selfish genes; theories of V. C. Wynne-Edwards and R. Dawkins. S. J. Gould.

New Yorker. 55:83–9. F. 26, '79. Our far-flung correspondents: manatees. Faith McNulty.

New York Times. p Bl. Ap. 22, '78. Psychology clinic for disturbed pets sometimes puts the owners on the couch.

New York Times. p A2. Je. 5, '79. Indian state fights Delhi on cow protection law. Robert Trumbull.

New York Times. p D3. O. 28, '79. Beastly happenings on Broadway. Mel Gussow.

°New York Times. Sec. 5 p. 9:4. Mr. 9, '80. Study sees hunting accepted. Nelson Bryant.

New York Times. p 20. Jl. 19, '80. Defying odds and DDT, 2 eagles are born. Harold Faber.

New York Times Magazine. p 38–40+. O. 12, '75. Human decency is animal. E. O. Wilson.

New York Times Magazine. p 21–3+. Je. 12, '77. Pursuit of reason.
H. T. P. Hayes.

New York Times Magazine. p 38–42+. Je. 4, '78. New battles over
endangered species. Philip Shabecoff.

New York Times Magazine. p 18–21+. D. 31, '78. New debate
over experimenting with animals. Patricia Curtis.

New York Times Magazine. p 110–13. My. 20, '79. Animals that
care for people. Patricia Curtis.

Newsweek. p 28. D. 4, '78. Duty calls; New York's Canine Waste
Disposal Act. J. N. Baker and others.

°Oceans. 12:27–8. Mr. '79. Coddling trout: working the warm
waste water. Anthony S. Policastro.

Oceans. 13:12. Ja./F. '80. Dancing dolphins. Richard O'Feldman.

°Organic Gardening. 26:134–41. My. '79. Toward a backyard fish
garden. Anthony DeCrosta.

Outdoor Life. 163:10+. Ap. '79. Worst attack yet on hunting.
Richard Starnes.

Outdoor Life. 165:52–5+. Ja. '80. Alien wildlife: the wrong move.
George Laycock.

Outdoor Life. 165:10–11+. Ap. '80. Exploding the anti-hunting
myth (report by US Fish and Wildlife Service). Richard
Starnes.

°Parade Magazine. p 20. Je. 3, '79. "Best friend" best therapy?
Lawrence Galton.

Parks and Recreation. 11:18–19. D. '76. Infected playgrounds: a
doggone shame. E. R. Fillmore and N. A. Croll.

Reader's Digest. 112:160–3. My. '78. Animal facts and fallacies.
J. D. Scott.

Reader's Digest. 114:81–6. Mr. '79. Conversations with a gorilla.
Francine Patterson.

Reader's Digest. 116:181–2+. F. '80. Case against animal experiments. Patricia Curtis.

°Science. 194:162–7. O. 8, '76 Animal rights: NIH cat sex study
brings grief to New York museum. Nicholas Wade.
Discussion: 194:784–6. N. 19, '76.

°Science. 194:784. N. 19, '76. Animal welfare and scientific research. L. R. Aronson and M. L. Cooper.

°Science. 195:131. Ja. 14, '77. Animals and ethics. Marjorie Anchel.

Science. 199:37. Ja. 6, '78. Assertion of dolphin rights fails in court.
Constance Holden.

Science. 200:628. My. 12, '78. Attorney General and the snail
darter; Tellico Dam project and the Endangered Species Act.
L. J. Carter.

°Science. 201:35. Jl. 7, '78. Animal rights advocate urges new deal. Constance Holden.

Science. 207:543–5. F. 1, '80. Symbolic communication between two pigeons (colomba livia domestica). Robert Epstein and others.

Science. 207:663–4. F. 8, '80. Sound playback experiments with southern right whales (eubalaena australis). C. W. Clark and J. M. Clark.

Science. 207:1330–3. Mr. 21, '80. Ape-language controversy flares up. J. L. Marx.

Science Digest. 78:36–43. Jl. '75. Between man and beast—the genetic-behavior connection. V. C. deKonigsberg.

Science Digest. 83:18–19. Mr. '78. Animals sense change before quake strikes.

Science News. 11:26–7. Ja. 13, '79. Whale of a song. Julie A. Miller.

°Science News. 115:202–4. Mr. 31, '79. Bloody harvest. Janet Raloff.

°Science News. 115:250–1. Ap. 14, '79. Food web. Julie A. Miller.

Science News. 116:372. D. 1, '79. Sea turtles dwindle as trade increases.

°Sea Frontiers. 25:130–9. My. '79. Communication in Atlantic bottlenosed dolphins, M. C. and D. K. Caldwell.

Sea Frontiers. 26:114–18. Mr./Ap. '80. Dolphin Project. Richard O'Feldman.

Sierra. 63:20–2. Ap. '78. Importation of animals: the unforeseen consequences. Gordon Laycock.

Skeptic. 23:47–51. Ja. '78. Survival handbook: Fido's rights and your responsibilities. James Makower.

°Smithsonian. 5:22–9. Jl. '74. In this zoo, visitors learn, though no more than animals. D. J. Chasen.

°Smithsonian. 7:52–9. Jl. '76. We must decide which species will go on forever. Thomas Lovejoy.

°Smithsonian. 8:52–61. S. '77. Animals and men: love, admiration and outright war. Kenneth Clark.

°Smithsonian. 8:42–51. Mr. '78. Noah's ark in tomorrow's zoo; animals are a-comin', two by two. Sheldon Campbell.

Smithsonian. 9:58–63. Jl. '78. Gorilla mothers need some help from their friends; studies at Yerkes Compound. M. A. Rock.

Smithsonian. 11:50–9. Ap. '80. Scientist helps stir new movement for animal rights. David Nevin.

Time. 115:50+. Mr. 10, '80. Are those apes really talking?

°U.S. News & World Report. 81:48–9. Jl. 26, '76. 100 million dogs and cats—Congress takes aim at pet population explosion.

U.S. News & World Report. 84:62–5. Ap. 17, '78. Preserving wild-life—a worldwide struggle; creatures under threat of extinction.

°Vital Speeches of the Day. 43:81–6. N. 15, '76. On the Christian love of animals; the worst of us is better than the best of them. Address, O. 21 '76. J. V. Schall.

Vital Speeches. 44:264–7. F. 15, '78. Different kind of captivity; address, O. '77. W. G. Conway.

Washington Post. 4:9. Ap. 30, '78. The movement for animal rights. R. D. Lyons.

°Washington Post. p N3. O. 22, '78. Wildlife is moving into the cities. R. C. Toth.

°Washington Post. p B1. F. 20, '79. Behavior mod, down on the farm. Beth Nissen.

°Washington Post. p M15. Ap. 22, '79. Students take to the wild in search of man's closest relatives. Lois Timnick.

°Washington Post. p A1. Jl. 31, '79. In sea rescues, the eagle eyes are pigeons. G. C. Wilson.

°Washington Post. p E1–2. Ag. 19, '79. Leave it to the beavers? Not by a dam site. Robert Treuer.

°Washington Post Magazine. p 19+. Jl. 8, '79. The beastly harvest. Margot Hornblower.

World health. p 3–29. O. '78. Animals and man: symposium.

N 15 80 3269-0.

The Reference Shelf

Titles of Related Interest:

Human Life: Controversies & Concerns (1979)

Land Use in the United States (1971)

Ocean Environment (1977)

Priorities for Survival (1972)

Protecting Our Environment (1970)

Women and Men (1977)

For a complete list of titles in print, write:
Reference Shelf, c/o The H.W. Wilson Company,
950 University Avenue, Bronx, New York 10452